I'll Be There...

A Story of Family, Friends, and Faith

Cynthia Eckhart

I'll Be There...
Copyright © 2024 by Cynthia Eckhart

All rights reserved. No part of this publication may be reproduced, distributed, or transmitted in any form or by any means, including photocopying, recording, or other electronic or mechanical methods, without the prior written permission of the author, except in the case of brief quotations embodied in critical reviews and certain other non-commercial uses permitted by copyright law.

Library of Congress Control Number: 2024916462

ISBN
978-1-964982-41-0 (Paperback)
978-1-964982-42-7 (eBook)
978-1-964982-40-3 (Hardcover)

For Joey

*Endings always come too fast,
They come too fast
but they pass too slow,
I love you and that's all I know.*

-Jimmy Webb

Table of Contents

Prologue 1

Chapter 1   A Long Time Ago 3
Chapter 2   December 2006 Joey 5
Chapter 3   Deb 7
Chapter 4   December 2006 Getting There 10
Chapter 5   Growing Up Me 15
Chapter 6   December 2006 My Guardian Angels? 18
Chapter 7   Life Was Easy Back Then 20
Chapter 8   Grandmas 25
Chapter 9   Louie, Louie 29
Chapter 10 It Ain't Easy Being a Tween 32
Chapter 11 Life Goes On 36
Chapter 12 December 2006 Hitchhiking Thru Georgia ... 38
Chapter 13 Brothers 40
Chapter 14 Surviving High School 44
Chapter 15 The Wedding Daze 47
Chapter 16 Daddy Saves the Day 51
Chapter 17 The Big Event 54
Chapter 18 Growing Up and Out 57
Chapter 19 Les 59
Chapter 20 Friendly Betrothal 63
Chapter 21 Fun in the Sun 66

Chapter 22	First They Live, But Then…	70
Chapter 23	God Gives Us Strength	78
Chapter 24	How Can You Fix a Broken Heart?	82
Chapter 25	My Big Decision	84
Chapter 26	December 2006	92
Chapter 27	You Can't Fix It	95
Chapter 28	Or Can You?	97

Epilogue	103
Author's Note	105
About the Author	107

For Joey

Endings always come too fast,
They come too fast
but they pass too slow,
I love you and that's all I know.

-Jimmy Webb

Prologue

December 2006

I've been thinking about her all day, I fretted. But it was way too late to call her tonight. Tomorrow will be soon enough. I hoped. I prayed.

How had this happened? Why her? Why her baby? She's a good person. God wouldn't do that to her. And I know she is strong, but if it hurts me this much, oh, how hard it must be on her!

These thoughts tumbled through my mind, and I wondered if I could sleep. I wanted to go there and be with all of them, but especially to keep an eye on Deb. I knew how I handled my own personal tragedy, and thought maybe, just maybe, I could help her with hers.

But, as much as I loved my Mom, I had seven long years to prepare for her death. And besides, moms are older and are supposed to die, so you prepare for that possibility all your adult life. Deb's tragedy? No way to prepare for that. It was so unexpected, so surreal, the kind of stuff you watch on that movie channel that always makes you cry and you need a box of Kleenex and then you feel like an idiot for being so darn sappy about a stupid movie.

Deb's tragedy was real. As much as I wanted to believe otherwise, the news was so bad that I knew that it wouldn't have a happy ending. Deb was going to lose her grandbaby, her precious two year-old bundle of joy that they waited so long to welcome into this world. No matter how hard we prayed, I think that deep down we knew that God had other plans for Joey.

She had been so good about keeping me updated on what was happening, so when I didn't hear from her, and she wasn't answering her phone, my heart sank to my stomach. This could not be good. I usually enjoyed the ride on the causeway from North Padre Island to my school in Corpus Christi, but that day I didn't even notice the waves and the birds.

I arrived at school early that Monday. Upon entering my room, I turned on the Christmas lights, hoping it would change my growing feeling of doom. I tried to write lesson plans and get ready for the day, all the while anxiously watching the clock. When it finally read eight o'clock, I was relieved. *Good, she lives in North Carolina and I'm in Texas She would be awake by now.*

She answered fairly quickly. I was afraid to ask her what I knew I had to, *needed* to ask. "How's Joey?" I didn't think I really wanted Deb to answer the question, but I knew I couldn't function that day without knowing.

I heard her take a deep breath. She sounded so calm, that I saw my surreal dream coming true, right there in my science lab. Suddenly everything around me stood still as I held the phone next to my ear, waiting for what I knew was coming.

"Joey died just a little while ago…

Chapter 1

A Long Time Ago

I can't remember not knowing Deb. She was the sister I never had. We were always together, even though we lived several blocks and one major road away from each other. I have known her longer than I've known my baby brother, and now that I was approaching sixty, I realized just how long that was.

We have argued for decades over how old we were when we met. Being a year older, I have decided that my memory is better on the subject, since she was so much younger than me. I was two and Deb was only one when her grandmother and my neighbor's grandmother, who were friends from way back, enrolled the neighborhood toddlers into swimming lessons at the downtown "Y." Our life-long friendship started in that pool.

We didn't go to the same school; that major road was the dividing line between our two districts. Which, in retrospect, was probably a good thing, considering how school friendships change weekly! We did, however, go to the same church, and we both learned to ride bikes, so we were able to spend quite a bit of time at each other's houses. We became extensions of each family. We played pick-up sticks and jacks together. We even played "Cowboys and Indians" and "Combat" with my baby brother and the toy guns Daddy carved for us.

I think Debbie sometimes enjoyed being around my brother. She had one of her own, but he was much older, so Pete kind of helped fill a void. She not only was my "sister," but also my escape from my pest of a brother. I guess it doesn't really matter the how and whys of our friendship; we both have just accepted that it simply exists.

Don't get me wrong; we have always fought, as sisters often do. We have fought over stupid little things when we were young, once over one of her boyfriends, and even in later years, over politics. But there has not been one other single person with whom I have poured out my heart, cried with, hugged, and laughed with more than Debbie.

We don't even have that much in common in our lives, except our total acceptance of our friendship. We're often so much in synch that every time a popular greeting card company ran an ad on television, one of us would pick up the phone and call the other. We'd have a good laugh because the other had done the same thing but got a busy signal. We have been together in person or in spirit for every family celebration and tragedy.

I wondered how this latest tragedy of Joey's untimely death would affect her. Can she survive it? Can I help her, even though I would never, ever, have this kind of hurt in my own heart? I did not know, but I was certain that I needed to get to North Carolina.

Chapter 2

December 2006
Joey

I hung up the phone and just sat there, too stunned to think. I had called so soon after Joey's death, that I didn't even have the details to help me make sense of it all. But since when does a child's death make sense?

I never got to meet Joey. I wish I had. But I knew her through the pictures that were regularly sent to me by her mother, Les. She was so darn cute, and had the biggest, most humongous brown eyes that I have ever seen. Deb said she had an "old" soul, and that her eyes were windows to the world. My favorite picture of her captured that spirit. It was one where she was caught wistfully looking out the window, and that photo had often made me wonder if she knew she was destined to have a short life.

Les had a lot of difficulty getting pregnant, so much so that it was thought that she may never have any babies. Since she was young, she had said she wanted to get married and have lots of kids. It hurt a lot to watch her struggle with disappointment after disappointment, trying so hard to become a mom. So, when we found out that she was pregnant, I think we all decided that Joey would be her miracle child, and we all knew that Les had been blessed with the perfect gift.

Right after Joey turned one year old Les found out that she was pregnant again- with triplets. *Wow! Another huge miracle!* Joey wasn't put on the back burner, but everyone was so excited over the thought of triplets.

As with Joey, Les had a difficult time with her second pregnancy. She was bedridden for much of it, and seeing a ton of specialists to help her get through it all. The entire family really encouraged Joey to be a part of the process, and when the triplets were finally born that summer, Joey was as excited as the rest of us.

Things progressed in their oddly normal chaotic way until right before Thanksgiving. Joey had just turned two, and the "trips" were thriving. As with the way of kids, a stomach virus hit them all right around the time they were getting ready for the holiday. The kids passed it on to parents and grandparents, and probably would have passed it on to the turkey if it already didn't have bigger problems!

Around that Thursday, Les noticed that Joey's skin had begun to change, turning more sallow. A few hours later her skin had a definite yellow tint. Although they had all been checked by their pediatrician a few days earlier, as a precaution the doctor asked to see her the next day. But Joey got so much worse so fast, that she was immediately placed in the hospital. When the doctors couldn't figure out what was going on, Joey was transferred to North Carolina Children's Hospital at Chapel Hill. By that time they were all scared, and all they knew was that her liver was failing at a fairly rapid pace. Within a few days, Joey became number one on the nationwide liver transplant list, but none could be found. It was determined that her dad, Andre, would give part of his liver to his precious Joey, which hopefully would sustain her until a full transplant could be performed. But it was not to be, for as he was being prepped for the surgery, Joey had a seizure, and it was decided that she would not survive the operation. Only two weeks had passed since Joey got sick, and now her Mom and Dad had to make the difficult decision to allow Joey's short life to end.

It was right after Joey's passing that I happen to call Deb. Of course, she was too overcome to talk, and arrangements had to be made; people had to be called. I understood, and while I was "family," Deb had to take care of her own kids, husband, and the other grandkids. I would have to wait a while before I could talk to her.

How can anybody survive this? Why? Why, God, did this happen? Joey's just a baby.

Chapter 3

Deb

Deb was born in Kingsville, Texas, surrounded by one of the largest ranches in the world. Her mom worked at the King Ranch, and her dad was the area's fish and wildlife predator control supervisor for the Department of Interior. Shortly after her birth, the family moved to San Antonio where her dad became the division's supervisor for all of South Texas.

At some point in time, Deb's grandmother came to live with them in their small two bedroom house. Her brother was older and by that time pretty much on his own. Like many of us growing up in the 50's, another bedroom was added on to the back of the house. The one-car garage was turned into a den. Typical stuff in and around our neighborhood during those times.

Not long after they settled in San Antonio, Deb's mom took a job with the county agricultural extension office, something that *my* dad was really happy about. She became Dad's go-to person when he needed info on the latest bug eating his garden tomatoes.

A few years later, Deb's dad began to show signs of depression. In the early years that I knew him, he participated in family activities. But as time went on, he went deeper and deeper into depression, to the point that eventually it was just easier for him to remain in what had become his safe place, the den, occasionally coming out to interact with the family. I never realized he was ill until much later in life; it wasn't something that Deb and I talked about until I guess we were old enough to comprehend it. But, her dad always came out to say hi to me, and he didn't seem to mind the few times I stuck my head in the den to say hello. He had a quiet voice, and almost always had a smile for me.

Deb's mom eventually became the decision maker of the family. She loved her job, and if she was ever stressed about having to do it all, I never saw it. I loved when she would cook a pork roast that would smell so good when we got home from church. I always found a way to get invited to Sunday dinner on those days that my own dad was working and Mom would not be cooking a big meal.

Deb's grandmother became very hard of hearing. This added not only a lot of frustration, but also humor to the household. Deb and I decided she had "selective" hearing, and you never knew when you would be selected. She loved to sew, so she spent a lot of time in her room doing just that. She passed the skill on to her daughter, who tried to pass it on to Deb.

Deb didn't always have the easiest life emotionally as she was growing up. Her parents rarely raised their voices, and I think I was the loudest person around. As the years passed, her parents grew farther apart, and money became tighter. But she thrived, and even flourished, despite it all. She and her mom became close, something that my mom and I didn't do until I was old enough to appreciate it.

Deb and I continued to stay in contact during high school, although we attended different schools and had each made different friends. We managed to find ways to have sleepovers at each other's homes on a regular basis. I have to admit that I was jealous that she seemed to have a lot more boyfriends than me, but what the heck, I did learn a lot about what not to do in my pursuit of a boy. Somehow hers always worked out. Hers would give her flowers and candy, while mine would toilet paper my house and stick potatoes up my car's muffler. Guess I could pick 'em!

Deb married at a fairly young age. I was tremendously jealous. We had always promised that we would be each other's maid of honor at our weddings. But she would be getting married and moving out of state, and I wondered if she would come back to Texas for my wedding. She would just have to. After all, she was still had to be *my* matron of honor.

I have to say that I approved of her choice of husbands; they have been married for almost 40 years, and produced two beautiful kids. He is still as handsome as the first time I saw him, and his personality always makes him the life of any party. They have had many adventures together, but most importantly, Gregg loves my friend. He still gets sappy-eyed when he looks at her, even after all these years.

I had heard that the death of a child is one of the hardest things for a marriage to overcome. I prayed Les and Andre would find solace, and I hoped that Deb and Gregg would be able to grieve together, and that it would bring them all even closer. I wondered if I would say the right things to them once I arrived for the funeral.

Chapter 4

December 2006 Getting There

I was a little strapped for money at that time, but I just knew I had to get to North Carolina. I became almost frantic in my attempt to find a way there. It was two weeks before Christmas, and flights were getting sparse and expensive. I had already told the school that my "God niece" had lost her first born. My colleagues had followed the story of the triplets and always smiled when I proudly brandished pictures. So they were pretty sympathetic to Joey's death, and covered for me while I left for a few days during one of the busier times at school. But actually getting there proved to be almost a challenge that I wasn't sure I was up to.

I called my friend, Jill, and told her what was happening.

"I don't know if I am doing the right thing going." I was crying and trying to blow my nose as I spoke. Jill had become my local "sounding board" for some of my zanier ideas. She usually kept me from doing too many foolish things.

She paused before she spoke. *Uh oh, she is going to convince me not to go. Maybe I should think this through.* Jill finally spoke in that calm, rational voice that would send me on my journey. "I think you know what you want to do. What is your heart saying? If it is saying go, then go and don't worry about it. I think it would be a good thing for you to be there for her."

"You don't think I would be intruding?"

"Not at all. You two are so close that I would think she would want you there. Just go. Quit worrying; we'll watch out for things here."

I don't know if I ever told Jill how much she lifted the burden off my shoulders. I remembered parts of a scripture about giving God your troubles. I found it in 1 Peter 5:7, where we are reminded to *cast all your anxieties on him, for he cares about you.* I think that was what Jill was saying to me. Stop worrying and just do what you need to do. I was not an overly religious person, but both Debbie and I had our faith foundations laid early in life, so I knew that God sooner or later would show me the way. Little did I know the strange path He was about to send me on.

I finally found a way to get to Wilmington, North Carolina. The airport there was primarily a commuter airport, as was the one in Corpus Christi. That meant that I had to change flights in Atlanta. Of course, that was my LAST flight change. I had several layovers and airline changes just to get to Atlanta. And, after 9/11, that raised all sorts of flags. Here I was, a loner, flying before Christmas, changing flights more than once, with tickets bought the day before. Needless to say, my ticket was "flagged" for all sorts of security alerts.

I was nervous and anxious, so I arrived early that morning at the local airport, and after explaining not for the last time, the circumstances under which I was traveling, my ticket got processed. The attendant was kind enough to check my bags straight through to Wilmington, and I proceeded to the security check.

I presented my ticket and driver's license to the officer. Even at six o'clock in the morning, the line was long. I tried to remain calm as he began to question me.

"Well, what did YOU do? Get caught selling drugs or something? Boy, your ticket is a four star one!"

Not being sure what that meant, I just smiled wanly and sniffed.

"I am afraid we are going to have to ask you to go through this security line over here." By then, I was realizing that four stars in the airport line wasn't exactly the same as a four star hotel.

Some twenty minutes later, I was finally given my shoes back. That was the day that I learned to never wear bend-over-to-tie shoes on a plane trip! By the time I got myself back together, I had only about twenty minutes before my flight was due to leave. Being late is one of my pet peeves, so I always made sure I arrived early. Deb, on the other hand, didn't mind at all being late. In fact, I used to tell her we had to be somewhere a whole hour before we actually had to be there. Then we would only be "fashionably" late!

I should have known what kind of trip it was going to be at the security line, but being somewhat of an optimist, I thought that maybe the worst was over. Nope! Silly me, that was the easy part. The flight was delayed because of weather in Houston. I thought it was kind of ironic that I had to fly from Corpus to Dallas, and then to Houston before I could catch my flight to Atlanta. Anybody familiar with Texas could easily figure out that going 300 miles north then 250 miles south to get to a town 200 miles east of you, was a little overkill. It's a price you pay for living in a big state with lots of territory between cities.

My hopper to Wilmington was due to be the last one that night, and I was relieved that I got to Atlanta with enough time to stop by the restroom and get a soda to tide me over. I didn't pay attention to all the grumbling going on around me, and I was so busy looking for directions that I didn't look out the windows.

"Ladies and gentlemen, we are sorry for the inconvenience we are about to cause, but we are experiencing heavy fog throughout the entire East Coast. Many airports are closing, which means many of your flights will be cancelled or delayed. Please check with your ticket agent to see when your flight may be departing." The pleasant airport voice would probably not have to experience the wrath of some ten thousand people now stranded in the airport in Atlanta all night!

I made it over to my gate, and was relieved to see that my flight had only been delayed by an hour. *Thank You, God!* I silently prayed as I grabbed one of the few available seats. There, I waited, and waited….

To pass the time, the young girl sitting next to me began to tell me about her day. I was only halfway listening, nodding politely every so often, and all the while watching the board above the ticket counter. I did find out that she had been studying abroad in Ireland, and was going to Wilmington to visit her sister, who worked as a nurse in the city. She was very chipper, I thought, for someone who probably was having a longer day than me. *Was I ever that young?*

Finally, my time to board was getting close when we were directed to a central ticket kiosk. I should have recognized the long line as clue number three that it wasn't going to be pleasant. Twenty minutes later, it was my turn, and the agent told me that I was to catch a plane at another gate, and to hurry because they should be boarding soon. *Why didn't they put that on the board above the counter where I had been sitting forever?* I took off as fast as my suitcase could roll.

Panting, I make my way up to the gate, only to be told that the information was incorrect, and that the original gate was the right one. I ran back, thinking at least I was getting my exercise.

I worked my way up to the agent, only to be told that my flight had been cancelled an hour ago. I was totally frustrated and mad, and when I get that way, I cry. I found a chair and promptly proceeded to do so. Once I calmed down, I realized that she said that I would probably be rescheduled for the next available flight. Gathering my wits, I went back to the ticket kiosk to see when that might be.

The agent looked at my ticket. "We can get you on tomorrow night's flight," he said in his perfectly bored voice. I should have had some sympathy for him, but I thought my purpose for traveling superseded everybody else's needs.

"I am coming from Texas to go to a funeral in Wilmington tomorrow afternoon! That night is too late!"

"Best I can do…"

"Not good enough." By this time, my voice was raising. Of course, by then I was even more frustrated, so more tears began to well. I didn't notice, or maybe I ignored the tapping of the feet and the sighs that were coming from the line. I even blocked out the snide remarks I heard.

"Please, I have to…"

"I'm sorry. Maybe another airline can help you. Next!" And with that I was dismissed. I hoped I had enough Kleenex.

I found another chair, and tried to figure out what to do. I finally started down the gates to any airline that could get me closer to Wilmington. Nothing. Zero. Zip. Nada. I wasn't gonna fly to Wilmington.

The bus! I thought. *I can ride the bus.* I exited the terminal, conveniently forgetting that I would again have to have the four star security check if I re-entered. Guess I was becoming used to it.

There's one good thing about Atlanta's airport, it is a one-stop shopping kind of place, so I actually found a way to look up bus schedules. Of course, nothing was going to Wilmington. I got the idea of just starting all over and trying to get a ticket. I glanced at my watch and saw that it was already 10:30 P.M. All ticket counters were closed. I figured that they were all hiding behind closed doors because they didn't want to deal with any more hysterics. Undaunted, I saw a line forming at one of the counters, so I rushed over. It didn't take me long to determine that they were all trying to make international connections, but, hey, by that time I was willing to try anything to get an early morning flight. And I thought that maybe my luck was changing because a very pleasant agent was actually getting some flights scheduled.

But not to Wilmington. Thirty minutes later, my turn came up, but this time I was told that the earliest flight would be Saturday morning. That was even worse than the first one. I thanked her, and with blurry eyes, pondered what to do next. Several minutes later I wandered into the ladies' room. I found a bench and sat, too stunned to even think about what to do next. I had been up since four thirty that morning, and it was now approaching midnight. My eyes burned, and my brain felt like mush. Only one thought kept pummeling my mind.

How am I going to tell my absolute best friend in the world that I won't make it to the funeral?

Chapter 5

Growing Up Me

I wasn't named after anybody in particular. My mom liked the name Cynthia, and my grandmother loved Yvonne. So, my full name doesn't fit on most of those itty bitty electronic charge receipts you have to sign. As I got older, Mama only called me by my full name when I was in trouble. Therefore, being somewhat of a goody two-shoes, the people in my life usually called me Cindy.

My mom was born in Louisiana, and came to San Antonio in the summer of 1949 to help her sister out after her baby was born. Mom liked the city and stayed, got a job, and became friends with a lady that would eventually become my Aunt Titter. The bus stop that both of them waited at each evening was across the street from the fire station where Titter's uncle worked, so he often came over and sat with them until the bus arrived. Those two decided that my mom would be the perfect match for his son, who was coming home after being discharged from the Navy.

They were surely right, because my dad proposed to Mom on the third date, on my mom's nineteenth birthday. Being a careful person, Mom actually waited until January to marry him. That same year, in December, I was born.

Mom and Dad moved into our two-bedroom home right after they married. The first neighbors they became friends with were Jean and Manfred, and their baby, Johnny. Jean's mom, Grandmother Lacey, lived with them, and she had a friend nicknamed "Moey" who lived around the corner. Moey was Deb's grandmother.

Dad joined the fire department, and Mom got a civil service job at one of the air force bases. Things were tight, but Grandma and Grandpa were always doing things with us or for us. I had a good childhood despite suffering from asthma and earaches. Our house was filled with laughter and fun in the early years. My parents loved board games, so we played a lot of them together. The only hitch in our happiness was that Mom was sick a lot.

One time, while I was in first grade, I was picked to be in the school play as Mary, as in Mary had a Little Lamb. When told I would need a costume, I tearfully told my teacher that my mommy was in the hospital and the sheriff had taken my daddy away. One could only imagine where my teacher's mind went. A few days later, my teacher made a home visit, and was greeted at the door by my frail mom. Mama couldn't understand why the teacher was talking about not staying with an abusive man, and certainly one who hit her so hard she had to go to the hospital. The light soon dawned, and Mom started laughing so hard I thought she was going to tear her stitches. The actual story was that my dad and a friend were fishing at one of the hill country's lakes when my mom had to undergo emergency surgery. The hospital sent the sheriff out to try to find Daddy so he could give consent for her surgery. Being only six, I had the facts but not the whole picture. Mom promised to reimburse my teacher for the costume she had also purchased and brought to the house for me. I guess it was too funny for Mama to stay mad at me for very long.

My teeth were very crooked, and as a result the braces I had glued on didn't come off until the day before my high school graduation. I guess you could say that I didn't have a lot of dates in those days. Metal wires and rubber bands had a way of getting in the way of your "goodbyes!" But I had my share of loves. Too bad they didn't all share the same passion.

My first serious love had his first crush on a good friend of mine. When she began dating someone else, I was there to console him. We dated a few times whenever one of our parents could take us to the mall or to the movies. We also went to different high schools, so we eventually drifted apart. On my sixteenth birthday, my first playmate, Johnny, who lived three doors down, threw a surprise party to celebrate the momentous occasion. Instead of coming to my party, my "love" toilet papered my house. I knew then and there that the romance was over, and even if it wasn't, Daddy would never let me marry him!

Trying to find the one you are meant to marry when you are only eighteen is a formidable task. Although I had many dates, none held my interest for very long. I thought, at age twenty, that I had met *him*. He had just graduated from college and didn't know exactly what he wanted to do. We dated for quite a while, and although he didn't know what he wanted, he was sure of what he didn't want, and that was to settle down and get married any time soon. He did eventually ask me to marry him, but I thought he was joking, and he looked so relieved when I asked him if he was serious. We broke up shortly after that night, and he didn't get married until several years later.

I really wanted to discuss my serious lack of romantic involvement with my BFF, but Deb wasn't there. She had married the love of *her* life and moved to Georgia, where he was stationed. I figured she was busy becoming a mom, and didn't have time to hear about the boyfriend du jour. I wished I had heeded my inner voice and called her for advice. Life would have been much simpler.

Chapter 6

December 2006
My Guardian Angels?

As I sat in the airport restroom trying not to cry out loud, I decided I had better call the hotel in Wilmington to ask them to hold my room. I dug through my carry-on and found the number. I had told them I would be in late, but I was *really* late, and I was thinking that with the way things were going, the reservation probably went bye-bye, too!

I dialed the number, and pleaded with them to hold my room. "I will get to Wilmington just as soon as I can. Thanks, I promise I'll be there."

"Wilmington? You're going to Wilmington?" I looked up to see the young girl from Ireland that I had spent a couple of hours chatting with in what seemed like two days ago.

"I'm trying to, but so far it has been a nightmare!"

"Well, I just got a ride from this lady that rented a car. I swear it must be the last rental car in all of Atlanta! Anyway, she is going to Wilmington, and I bet she wouldn't mind another rider."

The car lady stuck her head from around the corner. "Hey," she said and waved at me through the mirror. "I have one seat left, but we are leaving in ten minutes. You are welcome to ride with us, if you wanna."

I must have had a strange look on my face because she grinned at me. "It's up to you, but I think it is the only way you are getting to North Carolina any time soon."

What the heck...I'm fifty-five years old and I have never done something stupid like this. C'mon, live a little. My little shoulder devil was really working overtime. I took a deep breath.

"Sure! Why not?" When I was little and did something idiotic that turned into a disaster, my dad would affectionately call me a "bucket head that ain't holding much water." That little devil voice suddenly turned into Dad's voice, and he was ranting big time.

Oh well, at least I was making progress. *What have I gotten myself into? I must be insane!*

Chapter 7

Life Was Easy Back Then

When we were little, life seemed to mostly be one big happy playground. We were friends that got to spend time together. We were included in each other's family activities. We thought those times would never end.

Deb and I became involved in the youth choir at church. We took to singing like ducks to water. That was a nice way of saying that we sang – a lot! I couldn't harmonize naturally, so I carried the main tune. Deb was the natural harmonizer. There wasn't a tune on the radio that we didn't think we sang better than the artist. We both had ukuleles and between us knew about five chords. We were adamant that we were the next great musical act.

Deb would often go with us to my grandparent's lake home, and we would spend a lot of time water skiing and floating away the hours. Eventually we would have to head home, and we would somehow coerce Daddy to crank up the radio to the rock and roll station. Invariably, one particular popular song would come on.

"I fought the law and the law won!" We would sing at the top of our voices. The car didn't have air conditioning. We had to sing loudly so they could hear us in the front seat.

Mom would holler, "Girls!" We would sing louder and with more gusto.

Daddy would shake his head and laugh. Mom, on the other hand, would shake her head and roll her eyes heavenward. I am sure we sang loud enough to be heard in heaven. I won't even explain what we did to "Hang on Sloopy!"

I often would end up at Deb's for a weekend sleepover. Our house still had only two bedrooms at that time, and I shared one with my baby brother. It was so much more fun going to her house than her coming to mine. Her brother stayed away from us. Mine? He would insist on being part of whatever it was we were plotting.

We spent time looking over fashion magazines. We painted nails, styled hair, listened to the radio. We took long bubble baths in her deep claw foot tub. We played board games, *Slap Jack,* and *War.* We didn't worry about boys. Unless it was Elvis or Ricky singing their songs; then we would positively drool. This was way before the Beatles and Beach Boys! could have become one. He was an accomplished violinist, who could also play the piano and trumpet. Daddy was a member of the Junior Symphony in San Antonio, and was always performing as a child. But there was one huge obstacle standing in the way of Grandma's dream. She may have wanted him to be the next virtuoso, but Daddy only wanted to play the "fiddle." Grandma tried to teach me instead, but after a few attempts at bowing and screeching, she gave up.

I was very close to my Grandma, and was devastated when she died when I was only twelve. There is not a week that goes by that I don't think of something that reminds me of her.

Deb's grandmother's real name was Gertrude Olive, but everybody called her Moey. She moved in with the family shortly after they had relocated to San Antonio. I never saw her in anything but a dress, and most of them she made. She could really turn a fine stitch.

She considered herself a lady and was not above reminding us that even though we were little, we should consider ourselves the same. She would stop in Deb's room to say something then move on to the kitchen for tea. Her room was off limits, which made it even more tempting for two little snoops. Even though we realized that ladies would never intrude, we once stepped in when Moey was off somewhere. It was a small room, and the bed took most of the space. There was a beautiful quilt spread on it, one she must have made herself. Deb and I both felt guilty about going into her sanctuary, so after a quick peek, we scrammed back into our room, hoping that Moey would never learn of our discretion.

Deb also came from a long line of pioneer settlers in Texas that went back to the time of the Republic before statehood. Women were strong by necessity and tough by choice. I had an Aunt Prudie that owned a large spread outside Sonora, and at age ninety she still ran the ranch. Each day she would strap on her six-gun, stick a few cigarillos in her pocket, and ride her horse to check fence lines. I shudder to think what she might have done if she ran into a rustler.

Moey was no different. She may have thought of herself as a lady, but her West Texas blood ran deep and strong. She had grown up in a harsh land and had survived the dust and tumbleweed. Her stories were always entertaining. She once told the story of when her then ninety-year- old mother and she had a fight. The mom whereupon got into her jalopy, drove across the Mexican Border at Del Rio into Villa Acuna to the nearest bar, and proceeded to drink. She got so drunk that she fell off the bar stool and broke her hip! I don't think she was ever the same after that.

We also played softball. Back then girls were only allowed to play slow pitch, but we loved it! Our church started a team, and from the time we were eight years old, every spring Saturday was all about the game.

I could hit and throw fairly well, but was not overly fast. I started out at third base, then a try at first base, and eventually ended in the outfield. I could throw the ball accurately, and our catcher could catch anything thrown her way. Deb was the catcher. She was quick on her feet, fast off the ball, and accurate in her throws. We had a couple of really good pitchers who kept most teams at bay. Another girl and I alternated as "clean-up batter", and I learned fairly quickly that it was much easier to hit the ball over the fence than try to outrun a throw to first base. Our teams always had winning seasons, and the same girls stayed together on the team for almost nine years. We dared any boy to think that he could outplay us. We knew he'd be toast!

We had a huge open area behind our backyard, so we often had pickup games with the rest of the neighborhood kids. We played until suppertime, all the while imagining that we were the next big Yankee star. We knew all the taunts and cheers, and we gleefully used them at just the right times. We knew we were the best and couldn't be beaten.

The back area was actually a big open plant nursery, so it had tons of roads and trails. When we weren't playing ball we were riding our bikes and playing *Hide 'n Seek*. Having several acres in which to hide, the game would go on for hours. We loved summers!

Those summer days seemed endless. When we weren't at the lake, we would convince one of the neighborhood moms to take us all to the local pool, where we would swim and jump off the diving boards until we were nearly unrecognizable under the wrinkles.

Sometimes my young and very good looking uncle would take Deb and me to the movies. He had this white convertible. We would get <u>him</u> to put the top down and "cruise" to the theater. Afterwards, we'd go hang out at the local hamburger drive-in. We thought we were pretty cool, in a convertible, with an older guy, even if he was my Mom's brother. Unfortunately, Mom banned us from riding in the car when he was driving. Something about driving too fast. We didn't think it was speeding!

One of the things that we both loved to do was to spend time at the coast. Sunning on the beach, looking for shells, the time was magical for both of us. There wasn't one part of the sand and salt water that we didn't totally embrace. We could jump waves and boogie board all day long. When we were young, neither of us had any idea how important the ocean would become to us as adults. Although it was on different coasts, both of us ended up living by the sea.

Deb once invited me to go on her family vacation to Big Bend. It was a long ride, and her dad regaled us with stories about the areas we were traveling through. He told us of important events that occurred years before. We had just crossed the Pecos River when I learned a history lesson.

"You know," Deb's dad began, "there's no law west of the Pecos." I had begun to think about the implications of that statement when I happened to glance in Deb's direction. She had this sly grin on her face. Before I could say anything, she grabbed me and pretended to "choke" me, telling me she could get by with anything here! We both started laughing so hard that we were rolling around the back seat, holding our sides, gasping for breath.

I got back at Deb on that trip without planning to do so. She was going through a phase where she thought she was going to be the next top model. I took a lot of pictures of her on the top of some boulder in different dramatic poses. When I had the film developed, we thought they were cool and marveled at my photo taking skills. Quite a few years later, we were reminiscing through old pictures, and we came across the photos. We had another laughing session that lasted quite a while because each picture would send us into peals of laughter. I had taken every photo of her posing dramatically like some great stage actor, but they were all from the back, and not at a flattering angle. Not a single one from the front! Well, at least the rest of the scenery was beautiful.

Yes, indeed, life was easy back then.

Chapter 8

Grandmas

I was extremely lucky to have known all four of my grandparents, and my great grannies from each side of the family. The stories and wisdom that they passed on to me makes me miss them still to this day.

Mom's parents lived in Louisiana. Grandpa Hamm was a log truck driver and was gone a lot, so he was very infrequently part of my life. Most of my memories of him were from pictures of us together when I was very young, and a few adult memories from when we went to visit him. Grandma and he divorced before I was born.

My first memory of Grandma-in-Louisiana, as my brother and I called her, came around five years of age. Mom and I rode the train to Lake Charles, and caught the bus up to her hometown of Kinder. I don't know which I was more excited about, the train ride or visiting all of my cousins. Grandma had ten kids, and almost all of those kids had a bunch of kids themselves. Many of them lived in and around Kinder, so there was always a passel of youngsters running around the house and yard chasing chickens or playing tag. Grandma was great with all of her "sha bebes," as she called us. She made every one of us feel as if we were her favorite grandchild.

As I got older, I was able to spend parts of each summer with Grandma. Several of her sons farmed around the area. I learned how rice was grown and harvested. I wiped windows with my cousin at the gas station and swam in the old lumber mill pond. My "older" cousin had a red convertible, and since the town wasn't very big, we would cruise around town several times a day just to see and be seen!

I also spent a lot of time pondering about my great grandmother, whom we all called Groma. She had a typical Cajun porch added to the back of Grandma's house which was her own "apartment." I think I was invited once to visit her room. Usually, when I first arrived, Groma would come out of her "house" and into the kitchen. She would pour herself a strong cup of chicory coffee, and proceed to tell us "Allo, I don' speak no English, no. Okay? Bye-bye." At age ninety, she and her "boyfriend" would get into his old clunky sedan and take a picnic lunch to the cemetery where their spouses were buried. They would sit under the tree and talk. It took most of the day since he only drove about five miles per hour, half on, half off the road. But the Cajun people are a happy sort, so the townspeople would cheerfully honk and wave to them as they passed, and nobody ever seemed exasperated by their leisurely pace.

My grandmother had a wicked sense of humor and loved to play the national pastime card game of Cajuns, "Bourre." One of her sons would constantly tease her just to make her mad when they were playing, telling her that he didn't have to cheat to take her money. Grandma would always rattle something off in French that all of us kids couldn't understand but knew it probably wasn't very nice. She loved dancing, laughter, and family. She lived every day to the fullest, and never looked back. If she had any regrets, she never showed them. Although uneducated, she was very intelligent. But she was also stubborn in her ways. One of the favorite family stories of Grandma was when she became Mardi Gras Queen of her nursing home, advancing to represent her home town in the regional competition. When the day came to crown the new queen, she found out that it was to occur later in the evening than anticipated. She got disqualified because that was past her bedtime, and she was not going to stay up late for a sash!

Groma died at age ninety-two, having never learned (and I think by choice) English. Grandma-in Louisiana passed away right before her ninety-ninth birthday.

Dad's parents had a much greater influence in my life. We lived in the same town so we saw them regularly. Both Grandma and Grandpa were born in the late 1800s on large ranches outside Bandera. While both of them decided they wanted to move to the city instead of becoming ranchers, they frequently went back to Bandera to visit brothers and sisters that still worked and lived on the ranches. We would hear wild stories of shoot-outs over pigs, chasing Comanches off their property, and protecting the homestead from raiders during the Civil War. Many of these stories came from Grandma's mother, Granny. Granny was born in 1865, and told us kids outlandish stories of the Wild West, which my brother and I ate up. We were mesmerized as she shared tales of all the things she saw and experienced while living on the ranch that family still owns today. As I would listen to her stories, I began to see where my pioneer spirit and independence came from. She, too, died right before her ninety-ninth birthday.

Grandma was one of ten kids, most of who lived to be in their late eighties and nineties. Pioneer stock, for sure! Grandma tried very hard to be a society lady, but her ranching roots always kept creeping out. She loved to tell the story of how she would jump into the old jalopy in her dungarees and chase the horse-drawn fire trucks just to see what was happening and if her husband was fighting the fire. She had wanted her child, my dad, to be a musical prodigy, and looking back, he probably Moey had a love/hate relationship with the phone. As her hearing decreased, or if she didn't want to be bothered with talking, she developed a unique way of dealing with the ringing telephone.

I would call Deb's house. Moey would pick up the phone before anybody else. Then, depending on her mood, the "selective hearing" would kick in.

"Hello?"

"Moey, it's Cindy," I would yell in the phone.

"Hello? Hello?" I could hear other voices in the background.

"Is Debbie there?" I wished I had a megaphone. "Don't hang up, Moey. It's Cindy!"

"Hello? Nobody's home!" The old-timey dial phones made a very distinctive sound when you got hung up on. I would sigh, hoping that Deb would call me.

Like my grandparents, Moey was a big influence on Deb and the woman she would become. She had a presence about her that simply commanded respect. She didn't ask for much, but I am certain she had a full life. Moey lived to a ripe old age. When she was no longer able to take care of herself, Deb's brother, who was living in Del Rio, moved her to a nearby nursing home. Moey called it "going home," and shortly after she moved back, she died. She never got to see her granddaughter get married.

Chapter 9

Louie, Louie

It is funny how dogs become such an important part of one's life. When my dad came home with an English setter pup, my brother and I were ecstatic. We had visions of playing and running all day long with our new family member that we had named "Sam." However, Sam had different ideas. He fast became our father's dog. He followed Daddy everywhere, and was content to stay by his side.

When he was a young pup, he was really funny and constantly doing goofy things. On his first trip to the lake, he ran and played fetch in the water for so long that we had trouble getting him to come back. He must've finally decided that he was tired because he eventually made his way back up to the house. Figuring he would need drinking water, Daddy filled a bucket and placed it on the breezeway. Sam came up to the bucket and started greedily lapping up the water. Pretty soon, he sat, but kept drinking and drinking. About thirty seconds later, as we were marveling at how much he could drink, Sam laid down on the cool concrete, still lapping up the water. It wasn't long until we all cracked up watching him. Not only was he lying down and drinking, he started peeing at the same time. He had the most blissful expression on his face. I kept waiting for him to belch!

Sam had a way of barking that communicated to every dog in the neighborhood to join the "conversation." After several complaints, Daddy decided that he had to cure the problem. He took the screen off his bedroom window and moved Sam's doghouse right under it. He chained up the dog so he couldn't wander too far. He also placed a bucket of water right next to the bed. That night, right after Sam started his nightly serenade, Dad threw the bucket of water right on his head.

To say Sam was startled was a big understatement. One yelp and Sam jumped back into the doghouse.

My brother and I knew what was going on, so we waited to see what would happen next from the comfort of our own beds. A couple of minutes went by and no sound came from the doghouse. We all did our Walton thing, and were yelling out "good-night" to each other. I heard Daddy tell Mama that the problem seemed fixed. The house got really quiet.

Right before we were nodding off, we heard a quietly muffled "woof" from the dog house. It was as if Sam had decided that he would get the last word in, but he sure hoped nobody would hear him. That set us off with another round of giggling. Sam had the greatest personality and at supper Daddy would tell us the latest goofy thing that dog did. When he died many years later, no one was as sad as my father.

Deb had a dog named Louie. He was a cute black and white terrier, but he was a one-family kind of dog. He loved Deb but tolerated me. I would have been offended except that I understood it, as that was how our dog was.

The name "Louie" would play an important role in Deb's life, but not necessarily in a good way.

When we were teenagers, the controversial yet popular song *Louie, Louie* could be heard on every rock and roll station in the country several times a day. The beat was catchy, and we all made up our own words to fit the lyrics of the song.

One evening, Deb was at her school's dance, and the band began to play the infamous tune. Like all the rest of her friends, her boyfriend and she went onto the floor to show off their dancing skills. Somehow Deb slipped, and her kneecap popped out of joint. She recovered, and none of us thought much about it until a few months later.

Deb loved to dance the ballet, and would practice her "plies" in her room as she listened to the radio. One night, "Louie, Louie" started playing, and out of the clear blue sky, out popped her kneecap again! Once the swelling went down and it was okay to laugh, we thought about the coincidence of the song playing when she had her accidents.

Again, a few months later, we were at a friend's house visiting and swapping stories while sitting in lawn chairs on the driveway. Deb got up to get a soda, and as she returned, a band several houses down began to practice. Soon, "Louie, Louie" began to trickle down our way. We all jumped up, yelling at Deb to sit down quickly before she again hurt herself. She laughed and proceeded to do so when suddenly the chair's webbing gave way and down she went! After we all quit laughing we remembered to check to see if she was okay.

Several years later I received a call from Deb. She informed me that she was going to have her knee operated on. When I asked what had happened, she related that she was jogging in the park when the knee just gave out on her. It had to be fixed right this time.

I only had one question. "Was there a car that happened to drive by with the radio blasting "Louie, Louie?"

"Ha ha, very funny."

I thought it was…guess she didn't think so!

Chapter 10

It Ain't Easy Being a Tween

Life and circumstances changed for both of us as we approached our teenage years. Our friendship was stronger than ever, and we often relied on it to help us get through some stressful times with our families.

My mom had numerous operations while I was growing up. I found out much later on that it was probably the beginnings of her slow-growing cancer that would eventually take her life. At first, it was nothing more than "Mom's sick again." But things changed dramatically for me in 1963. If Deb hadn't been there, I am not sure that I could have emotionally survived the turmoil.

The year before, my grandparents were involved in a minor car wreck. They were not seriously hurt, but a routine examination revealed that Grandma had a tumor on her kidney. Subsequent surgery to remove the kidney did not give us a lot of hope for a good outcome. Grandma began a steady decline in her health. Eventually, the drive to and from the lake for doctor appointments became too much for them, and it was decided that they should move to town and stay with us. The only problem was that we still had just two bedrooms in our house.

Mom and Dad decided a few months earlier that times were as right as they were going to get to make some additions to the house. We had already turned the garage into a dining room. It had taken us two years to finish because Mom had another hospital stay, but it was worth the wait. Daddy did a great job fixing it up. But now, he needed a garage, so we started building a combination garage and shop in the back of the yard. My parents had also determined that it was time that my brother and I each have our own bedroom, so the same people that were helping us frame the garage agreed to help us add another bedroom and bath to the house. But we encountered another setback when it was discovered that the entire back of the house was eaten up by termites, and we would first have to do an awful lot of repair work. It was about this time that Grandma and Grandpa came to live with us, and my brother's and my life would suddenly be turned upside down.

Because most of the back of the house was torn off, Grandma and Grandpa slept in whichever room was in the best shape at the time. Mom and Dad slept on a mattress and box spring on the living room floor. My brother and I made our beds on the trundle couch that was placed in the dining room. We had to get up and push the beds to the side so that we could pull out the dining table in order for everyone to have a place to eat breakfast. This was to be our bedroom for about six months. School became our solace since it was so frustrating at home.

My brother and I each had a different response to watching Grandma getting sicker and sicker. He decided that he didn't need to go to school to hunt and fish, so every day the principal would wait for him by the back gate of the school yard where he tried to skip out after recess. He also became so afraid that he would catch whatever Grandma had that he became very much a loner.

Me? I scratched. My arms, my legs, my fingers. I scratched until I had sores. Mama would wrap my arms in medicine and plastic wrap to keep me from scratching in my sleep. She even bought some long formal gloves for me to wear. It didn't help. I knew my Grandma was dying, but I wouldn't cry. I wanted everybody to think that I was mature enough to handle it.

I talked with Deb a lot on the phone, but didn't get to see her much. She couldn't come to stay with me because there was no room. And once Grandma went to the hospital for the last time, we were farmed out to neighbors who could get us to school. Days often went by before we could all sit down and have supper together. I was embarrassed that we were living like that, so I, too, began to withdraw.

Finally, one week before the assassination of President Kennedy, Grandma died. She had been in a coma for the last three weeks of her life. After the funeral, Deb came over and just held me while we both let the tears fall.

But that wasn't the end of my woes, for what I didn't realize at the time was that my mom was very, very ill. Not three months after the death of Grandma, Mom started losing a lot of weight. She couldn't keep food down. She was a petite woman, so the weight loss seemed even more pronounced. Doctors finally performed emergency surgery, and Mom remained in intensive care for almost two weeks. She would live, but I was so scared that I was about to grow up without the two most important women in my life. I felt like I was in limbo.

Three short years later, my Grandpa decided to remarry. The trouble was he didn't tell us until it was a done deed. I came in late from church and heard my Dad yelling. He never yelled at the dinner table.

"Here... tell your granddaughter what you did." Dad threw down his fork.

"I decided to marry again." He looked very old and small at the table.

"When is this supposed to happen?" I tried not to let the tears fall.

"Well, that's why your dad is so mad. I already married her."

Dad yelled even louder. "And tell her when!"

"December twenty-first." *My birthday. He married someone on my birthday?* I was crushed. I looked around and realized that "she" was sitting right there at our dining table. I tried to be polite as introductions were made, but I finally asked to be excused, and I ran to my room.

I frantically called Deb, sobbing while I told her what had happened. The next day was Christmas Eve. Deb had already made plans to spend the night with me. I was crying uncontrollably by the time she got to my house. Earlier, my new "grandmother" gave me my Christmas gift. She made this big deal about how she specially picked it out just for me. I graciously thanked her (at least I hoped it was gracious), and opened it up to find a purse. It was a used one with her initials on it. I looked up and showed it to Mom, and she had this not-so-pleasant smile pasted on her lips. I pleaded silently for her to just let it go.

Deb found me sobbing uncontrollably in my room. She tried everything she could to get me to stop before I made myself sick, but it was too late. I thought I was going to die. She ran to my mom and pulled her into Pete's bedroom. By now Deb was sobbing. "She is crying, and I can't get her to stop! I don't know what to do." Mom hugged her and told Deb just to give me time.

I was so close to my grandma, and I didn't understand how he could forget about her so quickly. I loved my grandpa, but I knew I could never, ever love his new wife. I even wondered if I would ever enjoy being in Grandma's house again. I am not sure when I fell asleep, but I do know that the only comfort I had that night came from my best friend's arms.

Chapter 11

Life Goes On

While I was miserable in my world, I didn't worry about Deb and what was going on in her life. It wasn't much better for her. Her dad was falling deeper into his depression and had all but withdrawn from life. He rarely left his room except to get food. Her mother became even more determined to show that she could handle being the bread winner and chief decision maker. I didn't even bother to ask Deb if she was okay.

We continued to spend as much time together as we could manage. Our house got finished, and I finally had my own room. Dad had built some shelves for me, so we spent a lot of time decorating them with record covers while playing our favorite songs. We would go to her home and argue about which Beatle was the cutest, and which one of us should be the first to date him.

It was during those days that I felt that Deb and I were in danger of drifting apart. It wasn't because we didn't care any longer, but that we were each developing into our own distinct individuals. She was becoming more interested in boys than me, and I wavered between trying to be like her and acting as the tomboy I still was. She would sometimes get exasperated with me when I didn't want to get my nails done or my hair restyled. So I tried to pretend that I liked talking about the latest fashions, knowing all along that my fashion would be whatever Mom decided it would be. I didn't want to lose my only true friend over my lack of "style."

Not long after Grandma's death and my Mom's near-death, Deb's mom started having her own medical problems. She didn't tell me right away, and I was too self absorbed to see it for myself. She finally told me that her mom was going to have surgery. Her doctor had found a lump in her breast, and the surgeon was going to remove it. Neither of us had a concept of a breast lump being anything else but just that, a lump. All we knew was that her mom was going into the hospital. And from our past experiences we knew that bad things happened to people in a hospital.

The day of the operation, I went to school, but came home as soon as I could. Deb had promised to call me to let me know how things were going.

The phone was ringing as I walked in the door.

"Hello?"

"It's *cancer!*" Deb sounded hysterical. "My mom has cancer!" She was now sobbing in the phone. I knew she was thinking about Mom and Grandma.

"Where are you? What floor?" I was beginning to cry. "I will get there as soon as I can."

"Please come!" She pleaded with me.

"I'll be there!"

My dad had just gotten home from the fire station and was taking a nap. I had awakened him, and he rushed to the hallway. "What's going on?"

"Deb's mom has cancer and she's gonna die and I gotta go be with her!"

Dad put a hand on my shoulder and softly said, "You're not going down there. You would only be in the way."

"But…"

"Tell her that we love her, and to please call when she gets home. We'll figure it out from there."

I tearfully relayed the message to Deb, and she promised to call. I crumbled to the floor and sobbed. I cried for my loss, my near loss, and what she was about to lose. Dad let me cry, and then hugged me, telling me it would all be okay.

Deb's mom underwent a mastectomy, and had a week's stay in the hospital. It took several agonizing days for the lab results to confirm that her cancer was localized and did not appear to have spread. Breast cancer odds were not good then, but she managed to beat them and remain free of the disease for the rest of her life.

I guess that was the first time that I truly understood the importance of family and being there for each other.

Chapter 12

December 2006
Hitchhiking Thru Georgia

It was that thought of being there for family that had me deciding to hitchhike with perfect strangers to get to Wilmington.

The car lady did, indeed, get the last rental car in all of Atlanta, judging by the emptiness of the parking lot. The rental company only had a compact car left, so we squeezed both our carry-ons and ourselves into the car. Irish girl and I drew the back seat, but by that time, I didn't care that there was little leg room. It was by then just a little after midnight, and we started off to parts unknown, at least to me! Car lady assured me that she and her friend in the front seat had driven this route several times, and she loved driving at night. I felt somewhat assured.

The night was foggy, and the piney woods surrounding the interstate seemed to grow in the night, like some giant monster from a cheesy horror movie. There was little talking; we were tired (except the driver, I hoped), and we were each into our own thoughts.

We had driven about two hours or so, and I had finally gotten my second wind. The driver was humming along to the radio. That made me feel even more comfortable, so much so that when she asked how we were doing, my devilish side came bursting out.

"Gee," I said, "This is just like some Alfred Hitchcock movie. One of us could be a serial killer, and none of us would know it!"

We all giggled....then dead silence.

Oh, no, they took me serious! They're gonna strand me at the next stop. I wished I hadn't been so impulsive. Irish girl poked my leg and nodded toward the front. The driver had shifted in her seat and was adjusting the mirror in order to see the back seat. The other lady began to lean in to see if she could see anything out of the side view mirror. I was trying not to burst out laughing.

It was totally quiet for about five minutes until the passenger asked, "So… how are we all liking this trip so far?"

Irish girl decided to use her psychology studies to really start messing with them. She quietly began to ramble.

"Why are you asking? Why do you want to know? Look, I paid you my share of gas money. Just because we are riding together doesn't mean that I have to share my innermost thoughts with you. Who do you think you are, anyway?" By this time her voice level had increased dramatically.

I couldn't hold it in any longer and the laughter began to bubble out. Irish girl started laughing. The stunned looks on the front seat riders suddenly turned into understanding, as they realized that they had been the brunt of a somewhat cruel joke, and they also joined in.

The ice was broken, and we all opened up and shared how we got stranded in the airport. The old adage about life being the journey one takes to get to your destination was becoming so true for me. I was confused about a lot, but crystal clear about this: I realized that God had sent me in the direction of that bathroom to meet these ladies, for we all had a connection.

When I told them why I was going, and about Joey, the driver told me that she was a nursing professor at the local university and had heard about her illness. The other lady was an emergency room nurse at the hospital where Joey was first taken. She was trying to get a job at the same pharmaceutical company that Irish girl's sister worked. It was more than fate that brought us together there in Atlanta.

We drove all night, and arrived in Wilmington around seven in the morning. We dropped off the nurse, and then drove to the airport so I could pick up my rental car. I again thanked her, realizing that none of us had stopped to ask each other their names.

I got my car, and on a whim, went by the luggage carousel, and there was my suitcase. It had somehow managed to get to Wilmington with absolutely no trouble. Shaking my head, I drove to the hotel, where they were holding my room. I took off my shoes and tried to go to sleep, but my mind was still going ninety miles an hour. I lay there thinking about how it was that we got to this point in our lives.

Chapter 13

Brothers

When you are little, brothers are necessary evils. You love them but would not really want to have them around most of the time. I am not sure which is more irritating, a much older brother or a much younger one.

I had the younger one. He loved to insert himself into our conversations. He didn't care if the bedroom door was closed; he would just walk right in. Since we had shared that same space for so many years, I suppose he still considered it half his. When he was very little, I thought of him as my little doll. Not that I dressed him funny or anything like that, but I would tote him around, feed him, and play baby games with him. His response was often to bite me, and then smile innocently at Mom when I started to cry.

Pete didn't like Deb and my singing. Of course, the more he griped the more we sang in his direction. One song in particular drove him crazy, so we used it as our secret weapon. It was all about Grandma in a cellar with her stove, and it involved a lot of "snot." So, when he wouldn't leave us alone, one of us would pull out our ukulele and start up.

"Grandma's in the cellar..." Strum, strum, strum.

He'd come running down the hall.

"Oh Lordy cain't you smell her..." We were very loud by that time.

He would push open the door.

"Cooking biscuits on her durned ole dirty stove...." He knew what was coming next.

"In her eye there was some matter..." We were getting to the best part!

He would stand in the doorway, feet firmly planted apart, with his hands over his ears. "YOU...ARE...DRIVING...ME...CRAZY!" He would then run out of the room ala some little rascal: "Moooom!"

Of course by the time Mom got to the room, the uke was put away and we would be looking at magazines, listening to the record player. Pete would stomp to his room while Deb and I high-fived each other. Another victory for the girls.

His favorite trick was one that he reserved for whenever Mom was gone. During summer vacations, it was expected that the chores Mom had listed for the day be completed before she got home from work. No big deal- except when you have a brother that is totally uncooperative, and worse, enjoyed it!

Mom would assign me to mop the floor, while Pete's job was to run the vacuum. He would always finish before me, and as I would go out the back door to rinse off the mop, he would lock the door and grin at me through the window. So, I would run to the front, only to have him beat me to it and lock that one. Of course, he unlocked the back door first so he wouldn't have to admit that he actually did lock me out of the house. I would try to fake him out, but he much better at that game than me! This would go on for several minutes until he would tire of the tormenting. I never won one of those encounters.

The first time I was kissed by a boy was at a dance held in our garage. Don and I wandered outside to the mulberry tree, where he planted one on me. I must have responded quite ardently because he gave me a compliment on my kissing style.

"Wow! You have a pucker that would suck the false teeth out of a moo cow!" I thought it was the most romantic thing I had ever heard. I opened my eyes, looked up dreamily- right into the window that my baby brother was looking out of, grinning from ear to ear. I got enraged and started running toward the house.

"Hey, wait!" Don pleaded desperately.

"I am gonna kill him! Moooom!" The romantic moment was gone, forever to become a fleeting memory. Pete still has not apologized to this day.

Pete did become my protector as he grew up. Not that I really wanted him to do so. He always managed to find something to look at in the front yard every time my boyfriend and I were parked in front of the house. He especially loved to open the door, flip on the porch light, pretend to study the night sky, and whistle a tune through the screen door. After a couple of minutes he'd then shut the door and turn off the light, repeating the whole game every five minutes or so until I finally came in. If one of my old boyfriends that he didn't particularly like drove by the house, Pete made sure that he was seen first. If it had been popular then, I am positive he would have used the two-fingered "I am watching you" signal. He was a true romance buster-upper.

One day I got home from school, and Pete began to taunt me. He started in his sing-song voice. "You're gonna get it. You're in trouble. The FBI came looking for you. You're gonna get it."

I did the sister thing and rolled my eyes at him. "Yeah, right!" I called Mom at work to tell her that we were home safely. Her response stunned me.

"I love you very much, you know that. But if you have done something, or if one of your friends has, you had better tell me RIGHT NOW!"

I was sweating profusely trying to think of anything that any of us had done, still thinking this was some cruel joke perpetrated by my brother. But it was true! The agents *had* come to the house looking for me, but not because of anything I had done. An acquaintance had applied to their agency and had used me as a character witness. They needed to ask me a few questions. Of course, Pete never did tell me that part.

Deb's brother was ten years older than us. He was in and out of their home until he married and moved on. He knew how to push our buttons. He would pick on us, and Deb would yell at him. He would take my glasses off and dunk them in the dishwater, telling me he would clean them for me. He would chase us out of the room until we would hide in her bedroom.

He did have two redeeming qualities. Even though he picked on us mercilessly, deep down he had a kind heart, and he truly loved his sister. He would do anything for her, including finding the right guys for her to date. One time, when he worked at a local mortuary, he introduced Deb to a young man who was working there for the summer. That young man became Deb's husband. But, anything he did to us was immediately forgiven by me with his single and unexpected act of kindness. After my mother died, I contacted him for a name of someone to carve the tombstone, not knowing that chiseling the stones had become a fairly successful side business for him. He took the information, went to the cemetery, and did the work himself. When I tried to pay him, his response was simple and heartfelt.

"You are my sister's best friend, and your mother was always kind to me. Please let me do this for you." I was touched beyond belief. I knew that Mom would not be disappointed in his efforts. *Family takes care of family.*

Chapter 14

Surviving High School

I got a car first. It was a 1950 Chevy Deluxe that I bought from my cousin for sixty-five dollars and a book of S & H Green Stamps. When she married, her husband took her and the car on a honeymoon to Cuba. I'd bet money the car had stories to tell.

Because the school bus didn't come close to our street, and the public bus took forever, I was able to obtain a hardship driver's license which mostly allowed me to go to and from school. On weekends, Deb and I would tool around the neighborhood, thinking we looked pretty cool. It may have been old, but it had a radio, so we were good to go! It also had a passenger door that would fly open every time I turned a corner. Deb quickly learned to hold on to it during those critical maneuvers.

Deb earned her license the next year and eventually got a really cute beige VW Beetle. It fit her personality perfectly. There was only one problem with it. Now that she had her own car, she didn't need me as much to get her to places. She went on her own, often to hang out with her high school friends, many whom I knew, but since they were now at a rival high school, we were rarely seen together. It really bothered me. Of course my little voice was telling me that I was doing the same thing to her with my new school friends, but that didn't seem to matter as much. Even though we saw each other regularly and talked on the phone almost daily, it wasn't the same. We had enough girlfriends in common to not matter, but it was the male acquaintances that seemed to pull us apart. I often worried that our long childhood friendship was in jeopardy, but I was afraid to voice the fear lest it became fact.

Because of the school rivalry, we didn't attend the same dances. For me, that was good because I didn't want her to notice that I didn't get asked to them as often as she did. She was everybody's favorite date while I was just considered a good friend by most of the boys at my school. Occasionally my old playmate, Johnny, and I would go out if neither of us had another date. But kissing him was like kissing my brother Pete!

One summer, Deb's cousins were visiting from Washington, D.C., and were staying at Fort Sam Houston. As such, they had swimming privileges at the Officer's Club. They invited Deb and me to be their guests. I had met her cousins before, and they were a lot of fun to be around. I eagerly accepted.

We had been at the pool for a couple of hours when I noticed that Deb was paying particular attention to a slightly older boy. I was further amazed that she was having a great time talking with him. *Dang, she's good! Doesn't go anywhere without finding somebody to talk to. Wish I was that brave.*

She finally got around to introducing me to him. His name was Gregg, and his father was temporarily stationed at the fort. What I didn't know at the time was that they had already met, as he was the young man that was working for the summer at the same mortuary as Debbie's brother. *Why didn't she tell me that?*

I truly felt like a third wheel as he made arrangements to pick her up to go to a movie. Even more strangely, it was obvious that Deb liked him, but for the life of me I couldn't understand why she had never mentioned him before. *Oh, well, summer's almost over. We'll all go back to school, and everything will be normal again.*

Except things were never the same after that summer. Deb was still seeing her on-again-off-again boyfriend from school, which meant less time for us to spend together. Gregg had since been shipped to Vietnam. I didn't even think of him as dating material because he was no longer in town. But unbeknownst to me, Deb and Gregg were regularly exchanging letters. He was courting her long distance, and she never said a word. *What kind of friend wouldn't share that with her best friend? Am I not the one anymore?*

I graduated from high school a year before Deb and in September enrolled at the local community college. Deb followed the next year.

Our schedules and studies seldom allowed our paths to cross. But we saw each other at church and whenever we could find the time to get together. If we noticed that we were not doing as many of the things we used to do, neither of us brought it up. I continued my business studies, and Deb was leaning toward nursing. I knew that she was no longer with her high school boyfriend, and as far as I knew we were both playing the field, looking for Mr. Right.

A few months later, Gregg's tour was over, and he made his way back to San Antonio. He began to spend more and more time with Deb, which meant less and less time with me. Little did I know that their relationship had progressed to a full-blown romance. She kept that part a secret. I didn't know they were serious until he had asked her to marry him.

Chapter 15

The Wedding Daze

I didn't know what I was angrier about…the fact that she was getting married and moving away, or the hurt feeling I had because my best friend conveniently forgot to tell me she had found the one she wanted to marry. What I do know is that we had a terrible falling out. It was so bad that for the first time in our lives we were not speaking to each other.

Since we were very young we had planned to be each other's maid of honor. We had looked at wedding dresses in magazines. We talked colors, hair, and flowers. It was just understood by everybody involved that it would happen. Of course, when you were not speaking, it was hard to make plans when the real deal comes around!

I guess Deb asked me; I really don't remember. What I *do* remember was planning showers, making rice bags, and doing all the other maid of honor duties without yet having the chance to check out the guy to see if he was right for her! I vowed she wasn't going to take this serious step until I gave the nod of approval. Deb looked happy, but I wanted to form my own opinion. I didn't know why she didn't talk to me about him, and I was too proud to ask. So, we both went about our duties as if nothing was wrong. We thought we were hiding our anger well, but apparently as good as singers and ballplayers we were, we were not very good actors. Finally both of our moms decided that enough was enough.

My mom told me in no uncertain terms that I would not be going out that evening. I remember pouting a lot since I had plans, and she was wrecking them. Soon, there was a knock on the front door, and in walked Deb's mom, Granny, and an equally pouting daughter in tow. Granny, without saying a word, sat very commandingly in the chair.

Both Deb and I were doing the arms crossed, foot tapping routine when my mom joined in.

"Sit, both of you, right there!" Mom pointed to the couch. Mom was barely five-two, but she wasn't afraid of anything or anybody. Mom worked at Wilford Hall Hospital at Lackland AFB when the original Mercury 7 astronauts came through her office for medical testing. When she caught one of them rifling through her paper tray, she picked up a ruler and rapped his knuckles. The brave astronaut immediately stopped, and gave her a "sorry ma'am" and waited until she gave him permission to sit. So needless to say, we sat- at opposite ends of the couch- but we were not going to test either of our mom's patience.

Mom continued, "I don't know what is going on with you two, but this is ridiculous, and it is stopping right now!"

Granny lit a cigarette before speaking. "You girls have been talking about nothing else since you were four, and NOW you question it? Let me tell you what you two are going to do." She pointed at us with that cigarette. "You are to stop arguing and nitpicking. Cindy, you will be her maid of honor, and when you get married she will be yours."

My mom ended any discussion. "You two are best friends, for crying out loud. Stop this, because you will regret this for the rest of your lives. This WILL happen, and that is all there is to it. Do we make ourselves clear?"

Both of us hung our heads, refusing to look at each other. "Yes, ma'am," we chorused. We may have been mad, or embarrassed, or both, but we could still harmonize.

"Now that THAT is settled, let's talk wedding plans." Granny proceeded to explain what she had in mind for the bridesmaid dresses that she helped design. Mom took notes to make sure we had all the details.

We couldn't help ourselves and eventually started adding in our two cents. We unconsciously started inching closer and closer together on the couch. Granny and Mom grinned over our heads and left the room. We didn't even notice. Wise women, those two.

The weeks leading up to the wedding were stressful. Both of us wanted to have things perfect for very different reasons. She wanted the fairy tale; I didn't want to be mad any longer.

Deb had insisted that she style all of our hair, so we practiced on mine several times to find the right look. I was not very patient when it came to my hair, simple is simply better. But not Deb. She was turning out to be very artistic, and had suddenly decided that our hair would definitely be works of art. I felt the frustration build.

"Enough, already." I groaned. I could hardly wait to see what she had planned for my next torture. She had turned into some girly-girl and was getting more than a little upset that I didn't join in with more enthusiasm.

She sighed for the umpteenth time. "It wouldn't hurt you, you know, to put a little more effort into your looks." She gave me one of those "look what I have to put up with" frowns. I felt my foot tapping under the table. Fortunately, the potential groom arrived to visit his intended. I took a quick peek in the mirror. *Oh my God! I am finally going to have a real conversation with him, and I look like an idiot!* Suddenly, I was frantically looking for a window to climb out of when I heard him speak for the first time.

"Nice hair." He grinned. I looked at Deb. I swore if she could have done so, she would have given me a one-raised-eyebrow-I-told-you-so smirk. That would have been worse than any nanny-nanny-booboo! It was my turn to sigh.

"Thanks, I think." Thus began my first real conversation with her soon-to-be husband. I didn't learn a lot from him, but I did get him to admit that he liked Texas girls that had long hair, especially when the hair was piled up high on their heads. It seemed that he loved to take out the pins holding up the hair, one at a time. Well, he should like ours. We were Texas big with lots of curls and pins! *When was this wedding going to be over?*

The day before the rehearsal was the bachelorette party. Gregg's groomsmen had arrived from North Carolina. They were nice guys. Two of them were named Cozy and Todd. After having a beverage or two with us, they left for parts unknown, and didn't reappear until rehearsal time. I really don't remember what happened at the party, except for one thing. One of the bridesmaids had imbibed a significant amount of said beverages and couldn't keep their names straight. She kept referring to the guys as Tozy and Codfish! We tried to finish up the rice bags, but the funny thing was we just couldn't get those stupid little ribbons tied around them. I am sure there was much more rice on the floor than in the bags.

It must have been a heck of a party, judging from the headaches we all had the next day!

Chapter 16

Daddy Saves the Day

The rehearsal went off with very few glitches. Of course, in my experience, the rehearsals always go off with no glitches. The wedding day? That was a whole different ball game.

Thankfully, the groom and friends had gotten their tuxedos taken care of a few days before. They only had to go pick them up. Only trouble was, nobody knew where the guys were. Panic problem# 1!

Numerous phone calls to various friends and acquaintances provided no help. It was my job to keep them under control, but how could I do that when I couldn't even find them? It was almost time for me to go to Deb's house to get my hair styled. I did not want to be the one that had to tell her that her future husband and his best buds were nowhere to be found!

When the phone rang abruptly, Dad picked it up. After exchanging a few words, he left the house and drove off. Mom and I thought that he didn't want to be around all the drama. But, a few minutes later he showed back up with a familiar looking car right behind him. Out tumbled three very handsome but somewhat inebriated young men.

"How could you guys?" I deplored. "The wedding is only a few hours away. Where are your tuxes?" Panic problem#2 had just raised its ugly head.

They had the gall to look at me, then at each other, and start snickering. They were standing up, but I really thought if one of them had let go, all three would have fallen flat right onto my front yard grass. One of them finally pointed to the trunk.

"Give me the keys! Now!" I retrieved the tuxedos and groaned in frustration. *How was I supposed to get them ready?* "I swear, if Debbie doesn't kill you, I will!" I was really getting wound up to give them a huge tongue-lashing on how I couldn't do my duty as maid of honor if they didn't sober up immediately. They looked blissfully unaware that they were supposed to be listening to me and doing what I told them.

Dad shot me a glance. "I'll take care of it. C'mon, boys, let's go around back. I got something that will fix you right up." I swore he was laughing at the whole situation. I wondered if I really wanted to know what the cure might be. I just kept praying that they would still be in one piece by the time the wedding started.

I ran into the house, grabbed my purse and keys, and yelled at Mom that I was going to get beautified. She yelled back, "You already ARE beautiful." Mom always knew what to say to make me feel better.

I was the last of the group to get my hair done. Deb had a vision of what she wanted, and she meticulously wound curls into my hair. She interwove pink ribbons that matched our dresses. My nails got painted. I hoped that I stayed "dolled up" through the wedding and reception. Deb was getting more nervous by the minute. When I was put together, I hurried to Granny's room to see if there was something else that needed doing. I nearly fainted when I saw that she was still sewing on Deb's wedding dress. I glanced at my watch and shook my head. It was barely four hours until the wedding. I guess Deb had inherited her tardiness from her mom.

She looked up. "You look nice," then went back to sewing.

"Thanks…uh, is there anything I can help with?"

"Nope, I got it."

"Are you gonna be…"

"Not to worry, I'll get 'er done in time." She concentrated on the dress.

When I got back home, I told Mom that I had discovered panic problem #3. We might have to be a little late on the wedding. Mom shook her head.

"How's Daddy doing with the boys?" I was not sure I really wanted to know. She told me to go check for myself, muttering something about the "hair of the dog." I ran out the door to the garage. I pulled up short at the door.

Daddy was sitting on a stool, drinking a beer. The three guys were playing pool, laughing, AND drinking beer. I glared at Daddy.

He winked. "Old trick. Well known among us that have been there! Quit worrying, they will get to the church on time, and they will at least be lucid. I am not guaranteeing full sobriety." He took a swig and laughed. I left, thinking he had better be right because Deb wouldn't kill them, she would murder ME, and there would go our friendship.

The groom was drunk, the bridal dress was still being stitched, and I was all "frou-froued" up. I had heard that things always happen in threes. I prayed that our threes were over and done with. Weddings were not all they were cracked up to be.

Chapter 17

The Big Event

The time had come for all of us to head to the church. Mom took me, and Dad followed the boys to make sure that got there in one piece. They looked relatively "cured." The church was decorated, the candles were ready to be lit, and the photographer was waiting for his cue. *Maybe we are rid of the problems, since we had our three.* But I kept having this nagging feeling that something wasn't right. After another fifteen minutes, I realized what it was…the bride was now MIA!

I ran to the church office and called her house, but there was no answer. *O.K., breathe. She is on her way. She's just being late as usual. Don't panic!* Who was I trying to convince? Everybody else or me? Another five minutes passed, and I finally saw the car drive up. I rushed to the door to help, but nobody got out of the car. *Oh, God, she has changed her mind! Well, I ain't gonna be the one who tells him. What in the world is going on?* I was still trying to figure out what to do when the back door finally opened. I cringed in horror! Granny was still hemming her dress, with Deb in it!

Deb rolled her eyes. "We'll be done in just a minute. Still had a little bit of hem to finish up."

Okay…I'll just tell the preacher that it will be a few more minutes. I decided that this did NOT qualify as panic problem #4. It was just Deb being Deb— late and fashionably so! After informing everybody we were just about ready, and ensuring the groom's parents that the wedding was still going to take place, I hurried out to the car, relieved to see that the other bridesmaids were helping her to the bride room.

Did I mention we were a bridesmaid short? One of her good friends from high school had a severe case of juvenile diabetes. The excitement and excess food and drink of the past few days had caused her disease to really mess with her body, and she was rushed to the hospital. She would be okay, but it was too late for a "replacement," so we just added another usher. That probably would have been THE panic problem had I known about it, but I didn't find out until later. *Is this some kind of omen?*

It was time for the procession to begin. I took a quick peek in the church and saw that the guys actually looked sober, and they were even smiling. Gregg's father was a pastor in the military, and he was to perform the ceremony. He looked very handsome in his uniform and extremely happy as he watched his son. I looked at all of us, the fellows standing at the altar, and the rest of us in the foyer, each with our "forever" friends, and I thought that this was the almost perfect moment.

My turn came to walk down the aisle, and I prayed I wouldn't slip or fall. I turned to watch and swept at my tears as I saw her dad walking her towards Gregg. She looked absolutely stunning. It was worth all the planning and arguing.

The ceremony was beautiful. The music was setting the mood, as were the flowers. They looked perfect together. Everybody was smiling and crying at the same time. All the worries, the preparations- it was all worth it. *It couldn't get any better than this,* I daydreamed. It didn't.

It was time for the bride and groom to walk back down the aisle, arm in arm, as the newly married couple. My job was simple. All I had to do was help the bride with her train, give her the bouquet, and follow them down the aisle. Easy-peasy, right? Deb looked at me; I handed her the bouquet. She turned and started down the stairs before I realized that her heel was caught in her train. Fortunately, Gregg helped her and she made it down with no further difficulty. Like the good little maid of honor I was, I followed the happy couple to the foyer. I was happily grinning until I looked at the bride. SHE was seething!

"I've never been so embarrassed in my life! You didn't fix my train and I almost fell down the stairs!" The gritting of the teeth told me that this was a grievous error on my part. *It was an awful little train... and maybe it wasn't my fault. Maybe Granny missed that part as she was hemming.* But my little devil voice took over, right there in church. I blurted the very first thing that came to my mind.

"I'm *sorry!* I'll try to get it right the next time!"

Gregg threw up his hands and rolled his eyes. I suppose that was the moment he figured out what he had gotten himself into when it came to us. I knew I should have regretted my hasty words. *Friends were not supposed to talk to each other like that, especially at a wedding!* I tried to hide my hurt and my own anger over something so silly. But the one thing that Deb and I always had in common was our stubbornness, and both of us were determined to be the winner of this round! To heck with this being the bride's day!

The reception was held at a local private club. I got there quickly after the required pictures to make sure that the place was ready. Guest book, check. Rice bags, check. Flowers, check. Both cakes, check check. *Okay, duties are over with for now, thank goodness. Time to quit worrying and stop being mad. It's no biggie.* The band was playing, and I was going to have some good 'ol Texas fun!

After the requisite dances, I pretty much stayed out of Deb's way. I had decided that I didn't want to be part of any dramatics. As the party went on, I kept feeling better and better. So, apparently did my baby brother. He looked so cute and grown up in his tuxedo, but he was acting so juvenile! *What was up with that?* I beat him to the newly-filled punch bowl and was getting ready to tell him to quit messing around. Suddenly my dad again came to the rescue. He decided it was time to take my brother home before he got worse. When I asked what was wrong with him, Daddy muttered something about needing more "hair of the dog." It was at that moment that I realized that Gregg had secretly spiked the punch. No wonder I was enjoying the bash so much.

When it was time to help Deb change, I wondered if she was still mad at me. It must have hit her that her life was about to dramatically change, and she was leaving everything she had known and relied on her entire life. I knew that my support system was leaving, and for all I knew it would be forever. Neither of us apologized, but we realized that we didn't have to. All else was forgotten as two women hugged, resealing that childhood bond that couldn't really be broken. There may be distance between us, but we would always be together in spirit.

Chapter 18

Growing Up and Out

Deb had never been much of a letter writer. So it didn't surprise me when her letters were few and far between. I was over my hurt feelings and really missed not being able to just pick up the phone and call. Being on a very tight budget, daily long distance calls were not something I could afford. I would write and write, but for ever four letters I sent, I got maybe one. It seemed as if years had passed since I last saw her, even though it had only been several months. Her last letter to me was to share the news that she was expecting her first child, and I wanted to be a part of that experience.

One day my mom was walking to the car from the mall when she heard her name being called. She turned to see a very pregnant Deb and her mom, calling and waving. They stopped to visit a little, and Deb explained that this was an impromptu trip that was going to be quick and short, and in her excitement to see her mother, she forgot to call and tell me she was coming. She wrote down her mother's new phone number and asked Mom to tell me to please call.

When Mom passed on the message, I think I must have run to the phone before she even finished telling me of the encounter. I was so relieved that for the first time in many, many months we would be able to have a long conversation. I was also very glad to feel that I was not forgotten after all, because our friendship picked up right where it left off. I made arrangements to go see her at her mom's new townhouse across town.

We both were crying and hugging each other for what seemed like an eternity. After talking nonstop for several hours, Deb informed me that she was leaving tomorrow, as she had a doctor's appointment coming up in a few days back in Georgia. I knew it would be a while before she would be able to again fly across country, so I was bracing for another long absence. But she also had some good news. They were getting transferred to Texas, probably sometime the next year. We would be several thousand miles closer, and the thought that we would see each other much more often lifted some of the dullness from around my heart.

Five long months later, I finally received the anxiously awaited baby notice. She had given birth to a son. Almost from day one, you could tell who his father was, as he was a smaller version of him. I made my mom go with me to pick out the perfect baby gift. I was so excited and happy for Deb, and I could hardly wait until I could hold him. I was also feeling envious of her being a mom, as I had just broken up with the guy I thought I would marry. It was way too soon to think that my biological clock was ticking, so I decided that her son would tide me over until my turn came. One little problem with that…their transfer didn't come through the next year. I would have to be content with the occasional photo. Knowing how lax Deb was in the letter writing department, I wondered if I could hold my breath that long.

Bill was already two before their transfer came through, and I finally got to see him in person. He was already talking, looking more and more like his daddy every day. He strutted like him and even had the same mannerisms. The idea of a "mini Gregg" was hammered into my brain a couple of years later.

When Bill was four I drove up to Fort Hood in Killeen to visit for a few days, and Deb and I decided to go shopping in the next town over. On the way back, traffic got heavier, and it soon became stop and go driving. All of us were ready to be home, but I guess Bill was the most frustrated, judging by his outburst.

After starting and stopping several times, he stood up in the back seat, threw out both arms, and very clearly asked: "What the hell *is* this?" He sighed dramatically.

My eyes were round saucers, and I was watching Deb very closely, trying to be solemn when all I wanted to do was cackle!

Deb's hands gripped the steering wheel. "I am going to kill Gregg!" I started snickering, and couldn't even quit when Deb gave me "the look."

Maybe I wasn't so ready for motherhood after all.

Chapter 19

Les

Deb's daughter was born in Texas, so I was able to interact with her as a baby. She was really pretty and appeared dainty. But looks can be deceiving, for beneath that exterior beauty a stubborn daredevil was hiding, just waiting to escape. She was everywhere and into everything! I loved every minute I spent with her and her older brother.

Watching Deb with her two kids, seeing how she loved them without spoiling them, I really began to feel the maternal urges pop out. Once again, I was between relationships, and by then being in my mid-twenties really brought home that I should settle down and have kids of my own. My brother had just married, so I assumed that he and his wife Sherry would be the first ones to introduce grandkids into the family. In the meantime, Les would become my "niece."

It was a wonder that Les even survived being a baby. She had a habit of screaming her head off for quite a few minutes when it was nap time. Deb usually ignored her until she quieted down, and only then would she go check on her. That day was no different. However, after a much longer than usual crying bout, she went to check on her. Sure enough, Les had tried to get out of her bed but on the wrong side. She had gotten her feet down and was standing and pounding the mattress, wedged between the bed and wall. The only good thing was that she had cried so hard that once she was extricated from her predicament, she immediately went down for her nap.

A few days later we prepared to enjoy the Fourth of July celebrations that were to occur on post. Gregg's unit was in charge of the fireworks display, and as such, we got prime seats on the stadium floor. We had brought a picnic basket and mosquito spray, so we were good to go. We made ourselves comfortable on the blanket, waiting for the show to begin. Both Les and Bill were really behaving themselves.

Bill was having a great time running around the grass, playing tag with some other spectators. Les was in her carrier seat playing with her fingers and toes. Deb and I were sprawled on the blanket, contemplating the ways of the world. Finally, the show began. Everybody was clapping, oohing and aahing at the sparkling lights. Les didn't even seem afraid of the loud pops that were right overhead.

One thing that Les has always had is great timing. Right on cue, as we were at our most comfy stage and immensely enjoying the night, she started to cry for her bottle. Without looking around, Deb groped for her bottle, handed it to me, and told me to stick it in her mouth. Still looking up, I pulled off the top, and proceeded to do as directed. I was determined not to miss one single display.

A couple of seconds later, I heard Les choking. I looked over and realized that I had pulled the nipple off with the top and was attempting to drown Les with the milk. I discreetly fixed the mistake, all the while hoping that Deb didn't notice. I should have known that her mommy radar never shut down. Not even glancing over, she calmly asked. "Is she okay?" Her eyes were glued on the night sky.

I took a quick peek. "Yeah, she's fine." She may have been a little damp, but Les was now happily sucking on the bottle. I returned my gaze just in time to see the brilliant starburst right above us.

Deb sighed. "It doesn't get any better than this!" I had to agree. Good thing Les was too little to express her opinion.

I had the opportunity to visit Deb when they were stationed in North Carolina. Les was five years old and had just started kindergarten. She was so excited that first day. She wore a really cute plaid skirt, white blouse, shiny black shoes, topped off with a cardigan sweater. Her mom had pinned up her curly hair on each side. Les topped off the preppy look with her with her lunch pail and book satchel. I was not sure why she needed one of those. *How many books would a kindergartener have to take home anyway?* But that was part of the look that Les wanted, so she got it. She may have only been five, but she was already turning into a true "fashionista."

Deb and I whiled the day away until the kids got home. We took a walk, worked on some of Deb's crafts, anything to get Deb's mind off of the fact that her baby was going to school for the first time. Les had insisted on riding the bus, because she didn't want her mother there since she was a "big" girl now. While Deb allowed her to go alone, it wasn't without some motherly trepidation. Les had taken her very first steps to me, so I had claimed her has half mine. And because of that claim, I also felt some of the same fears.

As the time approached for the bus to drop off the kids, Deb anxiously kept peering out the window. *Aww, that's so mommyish!* I grinned to myself.

The kids finally arrived home. Bill was his usual happy-go-lucky self, but Les was another story. She was so mad that if the flames could shoot out from her ears, she would have set the kitchen afire. She stormed into the den, threw down her satchel, and loudly proclaimed her woes for the entire world to hear.

"That's just great!" Hands went to her hips, and she was patting her foot with so much zeal that I thought she might hurt herself. "That is just great!"

"What in the world is the matter, sweetheart?" Deb was struggling to be serious. I don't think I ever made it to serious.

"I have *homework*. Can you believe it? Me, a mere kindergartener, on the first day of school, and I have *homework*\ I can't *believe* my luck!" She proceeded to stomp off to her room. I was willing to bet it wasn't to do said homework.

Deb looked at Bill, who just shrugged. "You shoulda heard her on the bus!" He grabbed a cookie and strolled to his room. He was a seasoned veteran when it came to school.

We looked at each other and laughter began to erupt. I was not sure which of us snorted first, but when we started howling, we just couldn't stop. Bill, wondering what all the commotion was about, came into the room, stared at us, shook his head, and wisely left the room. That made us laugh even more.

A couple of days later it was really storming outside. It was fairly late at night, and we all were watching some scary movie on TV. Well, maybe it wasn't so scary, because I seemed to be the only one that appeared to be frightened. The kids were watching and playing, while Deb seemed to not be bothered by the monsters. But I had both feet on the couch and was biting nails. Maybe it was the tall pine trees outside the window, or maybe the noisy thunder, or both, but I was convinced that the aliens were going to enter the room any moment and take over my body. I was terrified!

Suddenly, without warning, Deb pounced. "AAAAAAAGGGHHH!" Her hands were zombie like. I am not sure what I did with the popcorn, but I am pretty sure I wet my pants. Deb had gotten me again.

I looked over at the kids. Bill was grinning from ear to ear, jumping up and down pointing at the couch. Les, on the other hand, went into her full dramatic mode. Not only was she laughing harder than her mom and brother, but she was holding her sides and rolling from side to side, her little legs one by one stomping on the rug.

When she caught her breath, she pointed her finger at me. "Mom got you good, Aunt Cindy!" *She called me Aunt!* I grinned happily.

Chapter 20

Friendly Betrothal

Les grew up, in spite of us, into a very beautiful young woman. She was popular because of her devilish personality. She was a cheerleader, prom queen, and later on, sorority sister. She had lots of friends. Deb decided it was time for her to start producing lots of grandbabies. I thought it might be nice if she found a husband first.

Les had a very good core of friends, many of whom were young men. One of them particularly held a place in her heart. Deb decided that he was the one she should marry.

Andre became part of regular family outings. He also considered Les his best friend, and neither of them wanted to do anything that would jeopardize that friendship. However, after seeing them together and the way they looked at each other when they thought no one was watching, I was convinced that Deb was definitely on to something.

Since becoming a teacher I regularly took advantage of one of the better perks, extended vacation time. I could stay more than a couple of days. So, Deb and I planned our visits around going to the beach to shell hunt and people watch. We mostly watched Andre watch Les and her watch him. Those two were in love but just didn't know it yet. One day Deb and I were again watching them frolic in the waves. She pushed her hat up, turned to me and smiled. "Those two would make beautiful babies together." I had to agree. He was as dark as she was blond and both were just perfectly fitted to each other.

Les would muse to her mom that she really liked him but didn't want to mess up their friendship. Of course, Deb wanted them together, so she would encourage her any way she could. Finally Les, having had enough of the razzing and teasing, would respond to her mom's pleas with a firm "Mom, stop. You are embarrassing me!"

Deb would stop, but everyone knew it wouldn't be permanent. She gave me a knowing glance. She wasn't going to encourage her so much, but neither was she going to *dis*-courage the budding romance. Those two didn't stand a chance.

I was also thinking of a time when Deb was the one hollering about being embarrassed; only it wasn't over a boy, but a movie. Deb, her mother, and I once went to the theater. It was a fairly funny movie, so the entire audience regularly laughed. In one scene the supposedly tough motorcycle rider was cruising down the highway on his way to confront the good guy. His hair was flying behind him, and since he was way too cool for a helmet, he had the wind blowing in his face, grinning from ear to ear. He suddenly reached up, and with his little finger, and picked his front teeth. Granny and I looked at each other and began howling. Hardly anyone else was laughing, and Deb kept telling us to hush. *Didn't anybody else think it was funny that he was picking bugs out of his teeth?* The more concerned Deb got over being "embarrassed", the harder we laughed. It was like being in church and getting the giggles. Once they surface, you can't stop them. I knew Les would have a difficult time stopping her "embarrassment," too!

Several days later, we decided to take an early evening cruise along the Intracoastal Waterway on one of the local party boats. The boat promised a tour that included a hefty dose of rock and roll music and beer. The locals called it the "White Trash Tour." Ready for a fun night, we invited Les and Andre.

We were having a blast, dancing and singing. After the tour ended, we were not ready to go home, so we ended up in one of the local hangouts. Several songs later, Deb and Les went on to the floor to dance, while Andre and I stayed at the table to rest. His eyes followed Les's every move.

"You know you're hooked, don't you?" I sipped my beer and studied his face. He looked appropriately miserable.

"I think I really love her, but I'm afraid I'll mess up our friendship if she doesn't look at me the same way."

"Oh, I don't think you have to worry about it. I kinda think she feels the same way. You guys are gonna have to talk sooner or later." I took another sip and hid my grin.

Deb and Les came back to the table. I announced that I was getting kind of tired, so we two older folks decided to head back home. After a brief discussion of how to get there without stranding the other, Les came up with the solution.

"You two take the car, and we'll get back home on our own. It's a small island. We'll run into someone we know sooner or later, and we'll hitch a ride with them. No biggie!"

As soon as we got in the car Deb started plying me with questions. She had seen me talking with Andre. "What did he say? Did he talk about her?" I could see the wedding planner about to emerge.

"Yep, he's got it as bad as her." Planning a wedding would be fun this time.

"I just wish they would talk to each other and get it out in the open," she sighed. "They are just meant to be with each other." I had to agree.

The next morning I plodded to the kitchen for coffee. Deb was already up, smiling serenely.

"Did you hear her when she came in?"

"No, was it late?" I felt better after my first sip.

"You could say that. They apparently walked the whole five miles back to the house along the beach. She told me they had a long talk, and guess what? She finally said it! She thinks she is in love with him."

Les came in about thirty minutes later. She looked pretty good for not getting much sleep. After a few sips of coffee herself, she looked at me and shrugged. "What can I say, Aunt Cindy? I think I got it bad!" She went off to go call him to see if he was up. Yep, she did have it big time.

Deb looked at me slyly. "I told you....beautiful babies!"

Boy would she be right about that!

Chapter 21

Fun in the Sun

Both our families had always loved water. We loved the power of it, and how it changed moods. We liked lakes and rivers, but we really loved the ocean. The waves are strong-willed and put you in your place. The calm surf hides the inherent dangers just beneath the surface. The water varies its color depending on the weather; it gives you a different look every time you see it. The seaside would play a big part of whom and what we would become as adults.

Which doesn't mean that we always acted like adults when we were at the beach. Somehow, the smell of salt water made us eight years old all over again. We always had adventures whenever we saw piles of sand.

Since we were little, our youth groups at church would make regular trips to the beach for a day of fun and sun. We would leave early in the morning and stay until almost dark before heading back home. We ate sandwiches made of baloney and more than just a little sand. Sometimes we'd cook hot dogs. In between there was wave jumping, sandcastle building, and lots of bird chasing. There were battles to be named "king of the mountain" in the dunes. We didn't care about how much sand was inside our swimsuits. The ocean always renewed both our physical and spiritual lives.

Deb was the first to migrate to the beach. The family bought a house in North Carolina on Kure Beach, on the Outer Banks. They were very close to where the Cape Fear River dumped into the Atlantic. Her kids grew up playing as we did at their age, and even as they got older they would come back, often bringing friends with them to enjoy the sun and sand. The house was always full of laughter and noise.

I was often able to spend vacations there, and on one such trip, we decided that much of our time would be spent on the beach. Before I left, I purchased several bottles of cheap SPF-15 or greater suntan lotion, thinking that I could slather it on and not feel too guilty about using so much. I had mentioned to my class towards the end of school that I had planned to go to the beach and just "veg out" for a number of days. I wasn't paying attention to the fact that one little girl kept asking me about my swimsuit. The last day of school her mom brought me a beach bag. In it were a visor, towel, lotion, flip flops, and the latest best seller. Then I understood the questioning, because the bag and its contents all matched my suit. It was a great surprise, and I couldn't wait to show off to Deb that I could "coordinate" when I wanted to. Of course, I wasn't planning on telling her it was my room mother's doing.

On the appointed day, we headed off to the shoreline, loaded down with enough food to last for several hours, chairs, umbrellas, boogie boards, and whatever else we thought we might need. Carrying all of our equipment became difficult in the soft sand. At least on Texas beaches, one could drive right up to the shore's edge, and the truck did all the hauling. *Oh well, at least the ice chest would be a lot lighter on the way back.*

Gregg was home for a few months, so he decided to come with us. He had this insane desire to become the "bronzed god" of the local beach. We didn't mind, since he very seldom minded our incessant conversations, and on occasion would even utter some profound words of wisdom. We staked out our territory, put up the umbrellas, lathered up, sat the required few minutes, and then dove right in. We jumped waves until we realized we were too tired and too wrinkled. Dragging ourselves to our camp, we flopped back onto our chairs. Once we had caught our breath, we reapplied the lotion and sat back to catch some rays. The radio was blasting, and we thought we were in heaven.

Time passed, and I noticed I was getting pretty red, so I again lathered up and put on a t-shirt. The red continued to creep along my body, so I moved my chair under the umbrella.

"Guess I haven't been in the sun for a while." I usually tanned quite easily thanks to my mom's Cajun blood and olive skin.

One eye peeked at me through her hat. Without raising her head, Deb mumbled, "You're not too bad yet." She went back to napping. Gregg was too busy singing to the country tunes to bother with any commentary on my predicament.

A short time later, my legs were really crimson, so I put on shorts, and moved further into the shade. Nothing helped. I now was pretty red all over, even on my feet. I huddled under a towel, no skin showing. The red kept coming. I was beginning to think I was allergic to the sun. *Gee, what a bummer that would be, having to be all covered up all summer.* I turned to Deb and Gregg and expressed my fears.

Deb flopped over. "You'll live."

Gregg looked at me, and proceeded to go back in the water. No sympathy from either one of them would be forthcoming.

The next day, the red was gone. Thinking it was just my imagination I shrugged it off and got ready for another day at the beach. I happened to use a different brand and I didn't get red. Thinking it must have been a fluke, I figured that maybe I had tried to make a mountain out of a mole hill. So I enjoyed the rest of my time and didn't worry too much about why I had gotten so red. The next time it happened, I just chose to ignore it knowing that the red would be gone by the following day. Once I read the ingredients of the lotion, I realized the problem. Many of the off brands contained aspirin, to which I was allergic. I was having a reaction, but at least it wasn't to the sunshine!

Several years later Deb and I again found ourselves at the beach. We didn't have boogie boards that.day; we had opted for inner tubes since there was hardly any wind. We floated for hours, solving the world's problems, reminiscing about the good old days, and generally oblivious to our surroundings except for the gentle breeze that wafted us along.

I got really hot, so instead of sitting on the tube, I decided to put it around me, legs dangling, but considerably cooler. It was fun riding the easy waves that way, and Deb soon joined me in a new adventure. Occasionally we could feel a small fish rub against us. We totally ignored the thought of *Jaws 10 or* whatever sequel they were up to.

Much later we noticed that the breeze had picked up and the waves were getting a little taller. Since we were pretty well pruned, we decided to head back in. It just so happened that the beach had recently been renewed with dredged sand which often caused the shoreline to have a fairly steep drop-off when you first step in. This was the case that day. What occurred next caused us to realize that we really were getting old, and no amount of wishing was going to change that.

We were pretty far out, so it took us a good five minutes to get close to the water's edge. Between the onshore breeze and incoming tide we struggled to stay upright. We didn't think about taking off the inner tubes. We walked toward the shore when it got too hard to dangle, still gabbing away. When we got to the edge, we started to take the big step up when a huge wave hit us from behind. We fell flat with our faces in the sand and our forty-something-year-old backsides sticking up out of the inner tube. We laughed, as was our custom when we got into these predicaments and started up and out again. Another wave crashed, and again our faces were buried, our derrieres pointing skyward. By this time we are howling. Every time we started to get up, along came a wave.

This went on for almost a minute, an eternity if you are the one being dumped every five or six seconds. Two young men were walking along the beach, and they noticed our predicament. They also were laughing, but somehow managed to gather their wits enough to come help us. I saw Deb finally crawl up on the beach with help from her white knight. My rescuer had just arrived.

Trying not to laugh, the kid said, "Ma'am, can I give you a hand?" Another wave, and this time he could not hide his mirth. I didn't know which made me more embarrassed, being called ma'am or having this young good-looking kid see my butt smiling up at him. He finally was able to pull me out of the water, tube and all. I was now laughing so hard that tears were running down my face. I looked over at my hero, and he was laughing just as hard as me.

When I finally caught my breath and took off the inner tube, I thanked him. He got up, dusted off, and still grinning told me, "No problem. Glad I could help."

I couldn't help but wonder if when he got old he would tell his grandkids about the day that he helped save a beached whale!

Chapter 22

First They Live, But Then…

As you get older, you become more reconciled to the fact that your parents will die, because that was a natural part of the aging process. It doesn't make it any easier for you to accept, but at least you are prepared for it. Sort of.

Deb and I were lucky that her mom's early bout with breast cancer and my mom's numerous abdominal surgeries didn't result in deaths for both of them. Our lives would have been dramatically different had we lost our mothers at such an early age. We didn't understand back then how important our moms were to us, and as we aged, we both frequently talked about mothers and how lucky we were to still have ours around.

Deb's father had been in depression and withdrawal for quite a few years. I think he was a little better his last few years, and he spent more time with his wife. But, I guess the damage had been done, and his heart, both the physical one and the emotional one, just wasn't up to trying any longer. When she called to tell me that he had passed away, I was not really surprised. He was to be buried at Fort Sam Houston National Cemetery, in honor of his service in World War II. I told her that I would be there.

The attendants were ready to lower the coffin, and guests were leaving when I noticed that Deb was at her father's side for one last time. She picked off a rose from the arrangement and ran her hand gently over the wood. She was softly crying.

"I never got to tell him goodbye. I wanted to see him just one more time." It was my turn to give her comfort. As I draped one arm around her shoulder, we just stood there quietly, neither of us having to say anything. Gregg gave us our moment together, and then quietly led her away.

My dad's death was also not unexpected. He had led a hard life as a firefighter. Having attained the rank of district chief, he would never send a man into any situation that he himself would not enter. He was proud of that, but it often put him in dangerous spots. Back in the early days of his career, the smoke eaters wore asbestos coats, and their protection masks were not very good. As a result, his lungs were shot. Add that to the fact that he also had seasonal asthma, and smoked, his lungs didn't have a very good future. I once asked him why he smoked, and he told me that it got the taste out of his lungs. He said that when a house burned, the smoke and residue left such an awful smell and taste that they used tobacco to get rid of it.

My dad died a couple of years after Deb's father. It was a few short months after my mother was diagnosed with terminal cancer. He had emphysema, lung cancer that had spread to the bones, and even a melanoma or two. He refused to even contemplate going to the doctor. I have often thought that he wanted to depart first because he couldn't mentally handle watching Mom suffer.

After Dad died, Mom began to think of her future and her illness. She made a decision in her mind, but I wished she had found a more gentle way to share it with me.

It was very late Christmas night, a couple of weeks after Dad's funeral. I was having trouble getting to sleep. Finally, a little after one in the morning, I had found that comfortable spot that allows a deep sleep. Suddenly Mom opened my bedroom door and said the words that would dictate my life's course for the next ten years.

"Are you awake? I think you and I should talk about you moving in with me. We'll discuss it in the morning." And with that, she left the room and strode to her own bedroom. *Am I awake? Well, I am now!*

The next morning after much discussion we agreed that I needed to move into the lake house with her. I was over forty, no longer in a serious relationship, and my apartment lease was up for renewal. The timing seemed right for me to move to the country and into the house that would ultimately become mine. Throughout the years, Mom and

I did not always see eye to eye on things, but the house was big enough that we could avoid each other if we needed to. Ironically, most of the furniture from the lake house that moved with me to my first apartment now came back home to roost. My brother and his good friend moved my stuff (not for the first time) back up to the lake. They both told me they hoped it was the last time they had to move the same things. That move began the best and worst times of my life.

When Mom was diagnosed, she was given six months to live. But Mom and her oncologist had other plans. The cancer had settled in the lining of her colon, and looking back, she must have had it for quite a while. That certainly offered an explanation for her numerous operations over the years. I didn't know what was in the future for me, but I began to realize that God had given me a second chance with my mother.

I found a teaching job nearby, and settled into life with her. We had a pretty good arrangement, especially the first few years. I would take care of the huge yard, and she would cook and keep the house clean. Mom insisted that I pay her "rent" each month, and I didn't argue because I knew she would just deposit it, and I would get most of it back upon her death. We did compromise and let someone come in and clean the house thoroughly once a month. That pretty much left the weekends for the two of us to do things together.

Mom grew up very poor, and was somewhat stingy in spending money. The only time she splurged was when she went to the grocery store. She had a habit of buying much more than she needed. Daddy told me one day that she did that because she had so little growing up. He told me he let her have her "Scarlett O'Hara" moments, as this was her safety net. She also had a habit of always looking on the ground when she went anywhere. She often found coins, and when she spied a penny, she would pick it up and tell me that someone was thinking about her.

When Mom was feeling good, we would go to the movies, or to some festival or crafts show. We often ate out, but we had to eat pretty close to home since we didn't know how her colon would react after she ate. I began to know my mother as an adult person, not just as my mom, and it surprised me how much I enjoyed the experience despite the fact that her terminal cancer loomed just over my shoulder.

The next several years, Mom had additional surgeries and stays in intensive care. Each time I wondered if this was it, the time she wouldn't come home. Thankfully, I had wonderful neighbors that watched out for both of us. If it weren't for Fred, Julie and Lou Ann, I am not sure how I would have coped. Fred and Julie gave me the physical help and Lou Ann gave me the spiritual nurturing I so needed. Deb was unable to spend too much time with me, as she was taking care of her mother, who had come to live with her, so I cherished the time that the neighbors gave me.

My mom was determined to live long enough to watch her grandkids grow older, so she really hated when someone would bring up the fact that there was seemingly no cure for her disease. That fierce need to defy the odds often showed up in very funny ways.

Living in the country, you get used to seeing all sorts of critters lurking around your yard. We had a flat rock at the end of our lot. Because trash was only picked up once a week, and we didn't want animals knocking over our trash can foraging for food, we threw our leftovers onto that rock. We all got a kick out of seeing which animals would eat what. Uneaten meat was loved by the foxes, but highly anticipated by the turkey buzzards. They had a habit of perching on our rooftop, making a lot of noise landing and settling down. For years, Daddy teased Mom and called them her "pets." She was never amused! Later on, when she was having a bad day, and if the buzzards were sitting there staring at her, Mom's reaction would be swift. She would find a small pebble and throw it at them, yelling, "Jerks! Go away, I ain't dead yet!" Anyone watching would laugh, knowing that spirit helped her tolerate daily chemo shots and monthly "cocktail" drips for so many years.

Six and a half years later, it was pretty obvious that her ability to bounce back was becoming much more difficult. The last surgery ended up with almost a month's stay in the hospital and a surgical wound that just wouldn't heal. I became more authoritative, as I figured Mom couldn't do for herself any longer. It became a problem since

Mom was not ready to give up on being in charge. We had quite a few "discussions" over that, and I realized that I came by my stubbornness quite naturally. When we got really mad at each other, we would both retreat to our end of the house and not speak for a couple of hours. Eventually one of us would start piddling in the kitchen, and the other would soon appear. The standard conversation would start off as "want some?" and the other would mumble "I guess," and the matter would be solved.

Several months after her last surgery, Mom decided that she wanted to take a trip to visit her brothers and sisters in Louisiana and Tennessee. We discussed how we could make it work, realizing that she would not be able to travel for long periods. We knew we would spend a lot of money on hotel expenses in between visits, but although we never spoke of it, both of us knew she was going to say goodbye to them. Money didn't matter. It was hard to watch her visiting with them, for they also knew they would never see her again.

Fourth of July weekend found my brother and sister-in-law at the lake house. They had brought the grandkids over to visit. Mom was now getting worse daily, and although we left it unspoken, we all knew that she didn't have much time left to spend on this Earth. She and I had discussed what had to be done when the time came, but I was really dreading it. Mama had been fighting for so long, and I was tormented. I felt tremendous guilt for wanting her to live one day and wanting her to just get it all over with the next. Her oncologist had told me at the beginning that cancer was a family disease that we would fight together until he told me that the fight was ending. I was afraid that he was soon going to tell me what I dreaded to hear.

The day seemed to go on forever, and Mom was too weak to try to get out of bed. She kept apologizing for the messes she made. Since I was little, I never handled "poop" and "urp" very maturely. Mom knew this, and was embarrassed that I had to clean up after her. I would go into my room and cry when I thought she wouldn't notice. My brother and I finally told Mom that maybe tomorrow we should take her back to the hospital. All three of us left unspoken that we knew she would never return home.

By the time we got to the hospital Mom's veins had started to collapse, so I had to make a painful decision to either feed her intravenously or give her morphine. I chose the pain killers; I knew I couldn't handle watching her hurt. The nurses on the floor all knew and liked Mom. She was very undemanding to the staff and so appreciative of what they did for her. They brought in a cot for me to sleep on. It was over fifty miles from the hospital to the house, so Sherry, my brother's wife, would spend the day with Mom while I went home and checked on the house. I would then go back to the hospital and spend the night. I did not want her to be alone. I began to treasure those evenings. Mom and I talked about anything and everything. We talked about her death, what she regretted, and what she was proud of. I told her of my fears, and even joked about her not coming back to haunt me. I said that I didn't want to wake up one night and see her sitting on the side of the bed. She laughed, and told me that she would drop me a penny every so often.

This went on for a couple of weeks. I started looking into hospice care. But I discovered that she was not eligible because she was not in the "active dying" phase of her illness. *Puh-leez! Are they nuts or something?* The doctor had already told me she would probably not go home. The insurance company was hesitant about paying hospital bills for palliative care only. I was really getting frustrated. Mom kept telling me it was okay, but it wasn't. Minutes before he died, I had promised Daddy that I would take care of Mama, and I didn't feel I was doing that. I was angry. Angry because I couldn't get just one of the groups to understand that she WAS dying. Angry and wondering why we paid all that money to insurance companies if they weren't there when you really needed them. *Oh God, it would be so much easier if she could just give up and go.* I would feel so guilty after those thoughts, and then I would get mad at myself for feeling guilty. Those feelings were followed by the niggling thought that I deserved a little consideration also. It seemed like a vicious circle. I needed Deb to help me sort it all out. But she was a month away from Les's wedding and taking care of her mom. I just couldn't ask her to come. We talked on the phone several times a week, and although it wasn't the same, it gave me some comfort and a chance to renew my emotional strength. She would let me cry and rant, and then offer some advice or story until I was able to again feel in control. She always ended our conversations with "give your mom a hug for me."

A few more days passed, and her doctor pulled me out to the hallway. He hung his head and gathered his thoughts.

"If I don't check her potassium levels, I won't have to do something about it." *What does he mean? What is he saying?* "Low levels of potassium slow down the heartbeat. It is a very peaceful way to go." It dawned on me what he was asking me to give him permission to do. The enormity of it all hit me.

"How long?" I whispered, not looking at him.

"Hard to say. Your mom has been a fighter for so long." He gave me the time I needed to process it all. I finally nodded and told him to stop checking it, just make her comfortable.

One of the nurses had given me a pamphlet on the stages of dying. One of the steps included anger. I had never seen Mom show anger in public, so I wasn't sure about that phase. I was about to find out.

It had been a tedious day. I had to mow the grass earlier that morning, and it took several hours. After cleaning up and driving back to town, I was tired and in no mood for another night of watching Mom breath all night long. I walked in the room and became rooted to the spot. My sister-in-law was standing at attention, mouth closed and eyes big. I called it her "pose." Sherry had been a highly acclaimed synchronized swimmer, and she assumed that pose right before their routine started. I looked at Mom.

She immediately turned to me and yelled, "And YOU were the one person I thought I could depend on!" *Oh, My God in Heaven, what is going on?*

I looked at Sherry then told Mom that I needed a soda. Sherry took the opportunity to skedaddle from the room. "Me, too! I'll go with you."

We both frantically stuck quarters in the vending machine and punched buttons until something came out. After a couple of calming swallows, she told me that Mom had been that way all day long. Nobody made her happy or comfortable that day. I thought about the brochure.

By early evening Mom had calmed down considerably. For the next few hours, she apologized to whoever walked into the room, even to the cleaning staff. They all smiled and spent a few minutes talking with her.

Her nurse came in and told me that they had found a hospice that could take Mom. It was decided that we would move her tomorrow since it was getting late. When I told Mom about it, she told me very calmly, "It's okay. I'm ready to go." I was relieved that we didn't have to discuss it any more. Thinking about it later, I believed she was telling me something entirely different.

The next morning, I arrived at the hospital thinking of all the things I would need to do to get her to her new place. Before I got to the room, her nurse intercepted me and gently told me that they wouldn't be moving her. *Now what?* I was ready to protest when she told me to go look at her legs and then come back out for a minute. I did so, and saw what she meant.

One of the signs of near-death was the pooling of blood in your extremities. It meant that your heart was shutting down and the veins were no longer able to move the blood around. The nurse told me that she probably wouldn't live through the night, and that I should call my family. Sherry was there almost immediately. Pete was out of town but was hurrying back as fast as he could. I called Deb and promised to let her know, and then I cried. I would be without my mom very soon.

Chapter 23

God Gives Us Strength

Mom had not attended church regularly, but I knew she had a deep faith in God. I had earlier contacted the pastor of our old church who had retired just up the road from us at the lake. He had spoken at Daddy's funeral, and I knew he would do the same for Mom. When it was obvious that Mom was not leaving the hospital, I called him to see if he could be on standby. But he had a family emergency and would be out of town for quite a while. The hospital chaplain had visited Mom regularly, but he was to soon leave his post and transfer out of state. I was at a loss as to what to do when the time came, but God again sent us a miracle. He sent another retired preacher that had served as a substitute pastor at our church. God sent us Pastor Mal.

Pastor Mal agreed to preside over Mom's funeral when the time came, but he was adamant that he get to know her before that time. So he began to regularly visit Mom in the hospital. They had long conversations that never seemed to take place when I was around. But Mom told me that she liked him and had told him of her final wishes. I secretly wondered when that moment would come. *How much longer can she hang on like this?*

I had waited for seven long years for her final moments, but now that it was happening, I wasn't sure I could handle it. We had been together for all of it, and now I was already feeling the distant pull of detachment. From the get-go, my brother had informed all concerned that I was in charge and what I said goes. *So, what was I supposed to be in charge of now?*

At mid afternoon, Mom looked at me quizzically. "Don't you go anywhere. Something is going on." I assured her that I would be right here. *Please, hurry, Pete.* He was not there when Daddy died, and he needed to be here for Mom, me, and for himself. He needed the closure.

By early evening, Mom was becoming less and less willing to join in on any conversation. Fortunately, my brother got there, and I gave him some privacy to talk to his mother. A few minutes later I went back in, and as I held her hand, she did something very strange.

"Why, hello!" Her other hand went lovingly down something only visible to her.

"Mom, who are you talking to?"

"Doesn't matter." She waived me off, never taking her eyes from her vision. "OK, I can do that." I was mesmerized. She looked at me, and then at her visitor. "Okay, then." *Was she seeing her angel?*

A few minutes later, she fell into a deep sleep, and we all knew it would be her final one. She would occasionally squeeze my hand, and I would quietly talk to her, telling her that it was okay to let go, that we would be alright.

Right before midnight, Mama abruptly sat up in bed, grabbed my hand, and very, very clearly said, "Help me! Help me!" *Please, God, please don't let her be asking me to save her. It's too late!*

I later thought that was the moment that God again helped me out. He put the words in my head that Mom needed to hear. I tightly held her hand and told her, "Mom, the only way that I can think to help you is to hold your hand. When you see Daddy, let go and grab his, and he will take you the rest of the way." By that time we all were crying. Mom visibly relaxed and leaned back onto the pillow.

Shortly after midnight, Mama went home. Each of the nurses came to her room and squeezed her hand. Some said a short prayer, while other openly cried. I was deeply touched and grateful that they got to see that side of my mom that I had so much come to love and respect. The thought hit me that I was an orphan. I was now truly on my own.

Pastor Mal met us at the funeral home two days later. By that time, several members of the extended family and some close friends had begun to stop by to say goodbye to Mom. I wasn't really paying attention to what was going on around me, but I began to realize that about fifteen or twenty people were sitting in a circle in the room and that. Pastor Mal would not let anyone leave. He told us that he want to hear "Mama Stories."

One by one, we each began to say something about Mom. As we went around the circle, the stories became a little more raucous in nature, and pretty soon, we were all laughing at some memory. We were an eclectic gathering, and each member of the group knew Mom in a different way. It was good to hear that so many respected her, and I was becoming even more aware of how much I would miss her. Pastor Mal used many of the stories in her eulogy, and it made the long day a little easier.

We all gathered at the house afterwards, and while I was glad to have them there, I was really wanting some time to myself. I had not yet really cried, and I wondered when I could have a good one. I was supposed to be the strong one, but I was tired- tired of being that and tired of pretending that I was okay with it all. I slipped into my bedroom, quietly shut the door, and sat on the side of the bed. I aimlessly looked around the room, and my eyes lit on a covered round dish on the dresser. Curiosity got the best of me, and I peeked under the lid and saw a cake. I had my first genuine smile of the day.

One of the things that Mom's sister, my Aunt Flossie, was famous for was her totally-made-from-scratch German chocolate cakes. For every relative that got married, her creation was demanded as the groom's cake. I had often teased her about when I would get mine, and she would promptly tell me "when you get married!" It had become a long running joke, with me telling her that perhaps she didn't love me enough. I now had my own cake.

A couple of minutes later, Aunt Flossie poked her head in my room.

"I put this in here because it's yours. I wanted to make sure you had it all to yourself. Now don't go sharing it." I hugged her, and I felt her tears. We just stood there. There was nothing else to say.

Mom's many friends and family lingered for most of the afternoon. I was more than ready for some "alone" time. It was turning out to be a very long day.

Finally everyone had departed, and I wandered around trying to figure out what to do next. But my mind was numb. Do I start packing her clothes? Do I stay in my room or move to the master suite, which was now all mine? What about all the bills? I aimlessly wandered around the house, looking for something, anything to do.

About eight o'clock, the phone rang. It was Deb. I just sat on the floor and cried, knowing that she was there for me. I don't think we said anything, but we didn't have to.

Chapter 24

How Can You Fix a Broken Heart?

Les was getting married a couple of weeks after Mom died. Mama made me promise that I would go and not worry about her. The last thing we did together was to pick out a dress for me to wear. She even decided that our gift to Les would be to ship some twenty dozen San Antonio-made tamales to North Carolina for the huge and getting bigger "pre" party that was to take place.

It was with a heavy heart that I made plans to go, but I needed to get away, and I knew Deb would keep me busy. Work was good therapy, and working on something for someone so precious to you was even better yet. I put on my smile and flew to North Carolina.

The wedding was beautiful and went off without a hitch. Les and Andre looked very much in love. Deb may not have gotten the fairy tale wedding she wanted, but her daughter sure did. And, as I thought, Deb kept me very busy so I did not have time to think about my loss. Three days of parties, get-togethers, and well wishes later, it was time for me to fly back home. I was reluctant to say goodbye. The last time I did that, it was pretty permanent.

Gregg carried my luggage downstairs to the car. Deb and I moved slowly outside. First we hugged, and then we cried. Neither of us seemed to be able to let go of the other. She told me it would be okay, with time, and that I should remember the good times, not the last few months. I knew what she meant, but I would never forget those times. It was etched permanently into my memory. Gregg stood quietly by, and I could have sworn he was swiping at tears.

Life went on when I got home, and there were even some good days. I was finding things to do with my new-found freedom. Not having to worry about Mom any longer was a huge weight off my shoulders, and even my heart began to ache less.

Seven months after my mother's death, the phone rang about five o'clock in the morning. I thought that perhaps something had happened at school and that I would have to get up earlier than I wanted. I did not recognize the voice and had to ask who it was. Whoever was calling was very quiet.

Debbie apologized for calling so early, but she wanted to let me know that her mother was in a coma and was not expected to live. Now fully awake, I asked her what happened. Granny had gotten some kind of infection that caused internal bleeding that could not be controlled.

She died the next day. I was glad that Gregg was home this time and not off somewhere overseas on a job. She would have somebody with her. When she called to give me the news that they would bury her in San Antonio, I simply told her, "I'll be there."

I met the family three days later at the funeral home. I tried to make small talk, but it was difficult. No one really wanted to hear it. It was obvious that she and her brother were taking it hard. They put on brave faces, but I knew them well enough to sense an act. I don't even know if I could have helped if I did know what to say. It was so close after Mom's death, and my pain was still obvious. Deb's heart was breaking just like mine did. The big difference is that I had a lot of time to prepare. It didn't really help, but at least I had it.

Granny was buried next to her husband. It was hard to watch Deb be in pain and not be able to help her. God had given me strength when I needed it, and I prayed that He would do the same for Deb. *Give it time, things do get better. I hope!*

Little did either of us realize that soon life would throw her a vicious curve. It might very well be the one that she could not catch.

Chapter 25

My Big Decision

After Mom's death, I began to question what I really wanted out of life. I was alone and would probably continue to be so. I could not bear children, and since I was turning fifty, I was contemplating if I even had that many years left. I tried to find contentment in my new role of spinster school teacher.

I really tried to count my blessings. Mom and Dad had made sure that Pete and I had a roof over our heads, both as children and as adults. Pete had wanted out of the city, so they gave him the ranch in Bandera as an early inheritance (they did make him ask me if I was okay with that!), and I inherited the lake house and property. I had a home, a job, and a little money in the bank. I should have been happy. Instead, I began feeling less and less fulfilled and more and more unhappy. I felt as if I was trapped in limbo, with no hope of finding the door out. You know, the one that God was supposed to open when the one behind you closed. I didn't understand that the door had already opened until one insightful day.

Mom and Dad had remodeled Grandpa's house to fit their retirement needs, and Dad had made sure there were lots of windows. His emphysema had progressed, and while he loved going out and piddling around in his shop, some days he preferred to stay inside and watch the world from within the comfort of his surroundings. He particularly loved watching the deer and squirrels. In reality, I thought he had a love/hate relationship with the squirrels. He had hung a bird feeder between two trees that could easily be seen through the window. He liked seeing how many different bird species would stop by. Unfortunately, the squirrels liked it as much as the birds!

There were over fifty oak trees in the back yard, and intertwined were a couple of wild grapevines that had wrapped their way around most of the trees. The squirrels would run and play up and down the trees without ever having to leave their safe haven. It was like watching Tarzan and Cheetah playing chase. But, when they made their way to the bird feeder, Dad would get more than just a little upset. He began to devise ways to keep the squirrels off the feeder. He first hammered tin squares on the sides of the trees to hinder the critters' traction. The squirrels learned to leap and land on the rope holding the feeder. So, Dad put a tin vent cover over the feeder. They learned to hold on with their back legs and reach under it. After much thinking, Dad put an empty plastic oil container over the vent to make it out of the squirrels' reach. They learned to leap from the tree and land directly on the feeder. On and on it went, with the squirrels winning every time. The "plan" became very elaborate over the years, and was a topic of conversation for anybody that wandered into the back yard. Even after my parents passed, I didn't have the heart to take it all down.

The combination breakfast/dining/den was his favorite spot. His chair was positioned so that when the front door was open, he could easily see who came and went. Many neighbors would toot their horns and wave to him as they rounded the corner. He'd always wave back, and then give Mom a narrative about where he thought they had been or where they were heading.

My epiphany came as I was sitting in that same chair. A neighbor drove by, honked, and as was the custom, I waved. I suddenly stopped with my hand still in mid air. *I am becoming my Dad. I'm going to grow old and die in this house. I can't stay here!*

I started thinking about the possibilities of selling the house. I asked my neighbors what they thought, and we spent many a night on the patio toasting the sunset and discussing the pros and cons of moving. I worried more than just a little about what my parents would think about it all. *Would Mom and Dad hate me? Would people think I am crazy? After all, the house was paid in full, and now, well into your fifties, you want to go into debt? This close to retirement?* Maybe I was a little "tetched in the head," as Grandma used to say.

I phoned my brother. I had all my arguments prepared. I knew he was extremely traditional and family oriented, but I hoped that he would understand my need to leave. After my Grandma died, the house didn't hold a lot of happy memories for me. My step-grandmother and I didn't always see eye to eye, and when I went up there as an adult, it was to mow the grass and check on my ailing parents. Besides, the lake was no longer the lake of my youth; it had changed, growing more populated and crowded. It didn't even seem as if we were in the country any longer. I was ready to tell him that I needed to be around people my age outside of school. I had even practiced being calm and organized as I laid out my potential plans. Pete never got to hear these arguments. What he said surprised me and stopped me in my tracks.

"It's your house. Mom and Dad left it to you to do what you want." I was trying think of what to say since he had just ruined my whole speech.

Finally, words came out. "But, how do you feel about it?"

"Sister, you gave up everything to take care of Momma and Daddy, and I just let you because I didn't know how. Whatever you decide, it's okay with me because you deserve it. I love you, and I will support you, whatever decision you make."

I needed time to think, so I promised him I would call him in a few days. I then put in the call to Deb. I knew what I really wanted to ask, and that was should I move down to the coast. I told her what Pete had said, and she told me that it was about time that he supported me, and that he was right in how much I had given up. I assured her I didn't think of it that way, it was simply what was done when you were the oldest child. I asked her about moving to the beach. I thought she might convince me it was difficult because of the many worries of storms, expenses, and inconveniences. Maybe I even wanted her to convince me I should keep the house. This idea was quickly mushrooming and going farther and farther outside my comfort zone. I was a steady, rule-following, middle- aged single woman. I never, ever, bucked the system or peoples' expectations of me. And there I was, thinking about moving away from everybody that I knew to live among perfect strangers.

Deb hardly paused before giving her response. "Well, it was certainly something that we both wanted to do ever since we were children. While it is a little hectic at times, I can honestly say that I really wouldn't want to live anywhere else. If you really want to do it, then do it! You will find a way to make it work. And quit worrying about what everybody else thinks. It is your decision alone to make." *That didn't help a lot; I wanted you to say yes or no. I wanted you to make the decision for me!*

A few days later I got brave and decided to let the other shoe fall. I called my brother. "There's something I forgot to mention. I was thinking about moving to the coast." I knew he had been thinking that I wanted to move back to town.

"*What?*" I imagined the stunned look on his face and thought that maybe this time I could recite all my reasons to him. After all, I had written them down, and they were sitting right there in front of me, ready to be checked off as I spouted them to him.

For once Pete was speechless. "Huh! Well, Sister, I guess you had better build a house that won't blow away with the first hurricane!" He laughed. "Actually, that might work 'cuz then I would have another place to go fishing!"

And with that, I gave up any thoughts of staying in the house that Grandpa built, and turned my thoughts to my first real adventure. *God, please help me out here. Am I getting in over my head?*

The House That Hurricanes Built Once everybody got over the shock of the announcement that I was moving to the coast, I began to make plans to sell Grandpa's house. I knew that was the key to me buying another home. I also knew I had to land a teaching job in Corpus Christi before anything else could happen.

I spent my weekends traveling up and down the Texas coastline looking for the place that felt right for me. I was pretty sure I wanted to build my own home, so I looked for a plot of land that was just right. Every time I found something, it was so expensive that I was beginning to think that I was indeed crazy to think I might make this work. I would always end up heading back to the lake with my frustration mounting. *Why can't anything ever be easy?*

It was toward the end of another fruitless weekend when on impulse I stepped into a real estate office on North Padre Island. There, I met a pleasant agent named Jill. This became another incident in which God led me in the right direction. Jill not only helped me find a piece of land that I could afford, but also introduced me to her husband, Ray, who financed it for me. Those two were the first people I met in what was to become my new home, and we have become good friends.

After a couple of trips back and forth, desperate to find a lot, I thought I had found it. But the owner withdrew the property because of an impending real estate boom due to the reopening of Packery Channel. Knowing that lot prices were about to explode out of my reach, Jill and I spent most of one Sunday finding a lot then calling the agent, only to be told that it was just put under contract. I was almost frenzied in trying to find any lot that would work. We finally found four different ones in my price range. Since school was starting the next day up at the lake, I had no more time to spend on my search. So, Jill suggested that we make a bid on all four, and take the first one that accepted. That meant her husband had to get me preapproved for a land loan on a Sunday, and that I had to sign four different contracts. Property was moving fast that day since the news about the channel project made the front page of the paper. We formed an assembly line: she printed up the offer; I sorted them at the printer, and then made copies. I gave this stranger that I had known for only a couple of days, four different earnest money checks. My heart was pounding, and I remember telling Jill "I'm putting my life in your hands here." She later told me my eyes were the size of saucers. Finally, one of my offers was accepted. It was actually the one I wanted, and with the help of long distance calls and a fax machine, the deal was finalized.

I was feeling good about putting the lake house on the market. It was then that the fireworks in the family began, and I discovered how deeply my brother's family roots ran. Selling the house was fine, but the things inside the house were a whole different ballgame.

I had decided that most of the antiques and furniture would not fit in what I had in mind for my new house. Realizing that some of them were well over a hundred years old, I offered my brother first choice on anything he wanted. I picked out a couple of pieces that I wanted to save; the rest would be sold at an estate auction. His reaction was somewhat unanticipated.

"You are selling your heritage!"

"I'm selling stuff. Who I am is my heritage."

"But some of that stuff has been in the family for years."

"So come get what you want."

"We don't have any room. I can't believe you would sell all that."

Back and forth the argument went. I explained that I would have to put things in storage, and that they would not fare well being stored for many months. And besides, I further explained that if a hurricane hit, it would all be gone anyway. When I told him it would be as if a tornado hit his house and everything was destroyed, he began to acquiesce. I convinced him I would rather the antiques go to someone who would really enjoy and use them.

"Well, I did tell you that it was your house and to do what you wanted." He sighed over the phone.

"Sherry and you talk it over. Decide what you want out of the house or the shop, and then come get it. The auction is set for next month." I wanted to get the emotional part out of the way.

The auctioneers were friends of mine, and they did a wonderful job of planning and advertising for the sale. Everything but a couple of small items sold. Even stuff that I considered junk became someone else's treasure. People would ask me about the history of a particular piece, or how old I thought it was. But the best conversations I had were about my Dad's squirrel contraption. They would just look at me, then at his attempts to beat the squirrels, and they would start giggling. It was a pretty funny looking sight!

There was one particular wall hanging that Dad had made that had our registered brand and other western memorabilia artfully placed on the wood. While it didn't sell, the spurs on it did. When I told my brother how much they had sold for, he was astounded!

"Eight hundred bucks? Are you kidding me? Man, I am going through my garage tomorrow." I knew then that he finally thought of it as "stuff."

I landed a job, sold the house, and moved to the island. To my brother and his best friend's relief, the furniture-moving was delegated to my niece, nephew and HIS best friend. I rented a small but right-on-the- beach apartment and spent many long days sitting in the sand performing one of my favorite pastimes, people watching. I began to look for a builder. I again lucked out and found someone trustworthy, and plans were made to start construction. Three weeks later, the foundation was poured, and the Gulf of Mexico became the focus of everyone's attention. Hurricane Katrina was looming large. We began discussing holding off doing anything more until we knew what was going to happen.

We waited, and fortunately for us but not so for Louisiana and Mississippi, the storm did not come our way. We began framing, and were just about done when Hurricane Rita took a bead on Corpus Christi. *Oh well, if it had to happen now, it's good the walls aren't up yet. Guess the tie-down system we are using will get a good test.* The city began preparations for an evacuation. Again, the storm curved and wreaked its havoc in East Texas and Louisiana. We were all thinking that we got lucky, and that maybe all the storms were done for the year.

We continued building. Half of the tiles were laid, and we were awaiting the arrival of the rest of them. Unfortunately, they were stranded on a truck that was stuck in Florida when Hurricane Wilma struck the area. *Is God trying to send me a message?*

I had been calling Deb, keeping her updated on the progress. I told her that maybe this wasn't meant to be, with so many storms threatening us since I started building. She laughed and reminded me to not forget where she lived, and how many times she had to evacuate. She said the first time a storm headed towards the Cape, she took everything she could get her hands on. The second time, she took a lot less, figuring the insurance she carried would replace most of it. By the third one, she only grabbed her jewelry, her evacuation box containing all the important papers, her computer, and the dogs.

"I promise you get used to it. If you worry about it too much, you will never enjoy the other months when no storm is coming. And besides, you yourself said it was only stuff, right?" I did say that, so I had to trust her that she was right about getting used to it.

Ninety-one days after the laying of the foundation, I moved into my new home. The first card I got was from Deb, and the first visitors were my brother and his family. He brought his fishing pole, and he and his son poured over maps in an effort to find the best fishing hole. While they were gone, we girls went to the beach and people watched. *Maybe moving here was the right thing to do to start my new life.*

A few months after I had settled in, doubts began to creep back into my mind, especially about spending so much of the money. *I just wish that Mom and Dad would give me a sign that they were okay with all of this!*

The next day I walked to the curb to get the mail, and right at the base of the mailbox were dozens of pennies scattered around. I was laughing and thinking about Mom's penny-picking. The next day, the same thing occurred. There were even more pennies. I grinned broadly because I realized that the coins had to be my pennies from heaven. Mom and Dad were telling me everything would be okay.

Chapter 26

December 2006

I finally met up with the family at the same church that Joey's parents were married in. *How different the church looks this time.* I had planned to sit in the back so as not to be in anybody's way. Some of Gregg's family saw me, and motioned me forward to sit with them. I ended up sitting between two of Joey's young cousins, and we held each other's hands during the service.

That morning I thought of the difficult journey that finally got me here. I thought of both of our moms and how crushed Deb's mom would have been. She would have put on the brave face, but we all would have known it was an act.

I saw Deb for the first time. She and Gregg were both trying to help Les and Andre get through this nightmare. I had only spoken to her on the phone, not feeling it was my place to go to the house. She would let me know when she needed me.

Joey's Uncle Bill gave the eulogy. It was so appropriate. He showed us all what she was like. He shared the good, and the not so good. Like her uncle, she had developed a colorful vocabulary at a young age. He had us all smiling as he told of Joey's ability to drop "s-bombs" as if they were "planned precision strikes." Apparently she knew it was wrong, because after laying it out for all to hear, she would immediately throw out the required "sowwy." *I wish I had gotten to meet her, just once…*

After the church services we were given instructions as to how to reach the cemetery that would be Joey's resting place. Going to the parking lot, I was able to catch up with Deb and squeeze her hand, promising that I would come to the house afterwards. Bill and his wife, Abby, were holding vigil over his sister and her husband. I gave them each a hug, again promising to stop by the house.

I ran into some old friends of Deb and Gregg, and they assured me that they knew the way to the cemetery. I should have known better. God had other plans.

It took several airliners, battles with security, and hitchhiking with strangers to travel the fifteen hundred miles from Texas. But it only took one wrong turn for the friends and me to get so far off the beaten track that by the time we figured out where we went wrong and got to the cemetery, the service was over. I had missed the final chapter.

⁓∞⁓

When I got to the house, people were milling around, talking quietly and catching up with old friends. Occasionally I would see one of them shake his or her head, as if they, too, were trying to make sense of Joey's death. I tried to stay in the background, knowing that I would have my "alone" time with the family. I busied myself cleaning up the kitchen.

Les's good friend joined me. After a few minutes of silence, I asked her what she thought of the graveside services. She hesitated. *She doesn't want to talk about it. It must be too hard.* I told her that I only wanted to know because I had missed the turn and got there too late. Her eyes widened, and she pulled me out of the kitchen and into an empty bedroom.

"I missed it too! I was trying to find a way to ask you about it!" We both hugged and smiled. I assured her that Les wouldn't mind, it was the thought that counted. I thought of the irony that good friends of both the mother and the daughter would each take the wrong turn.

Unknowingly, I provided the comic relief with my tales of hitchhiking. The entire family stood staring at me gape-mouthed at my description of the journey. There was a chorus of "no way- not you" from all of them. They must have been as surprised as I was that I would actually do something wild.

Deb, Gregg, and I finally had a few quiet moments alone. I expected their sadness and incomprehension. I had not expected their anger. It shook me to my core when they expressed their anger with God. *Out of all of us, your faith has always been constant. Why question it now, when you needed Him the most?* I remained quiet; I knew of nothing that I could say that would make any sense, and I wondered if anything would ever again seem normal for any of them.

I had to leave the next morning, so I said my goodbyes that afternoon. This time, it was me telling Deb that it would be okay in time. I think we were both hoping that it would. Just like my last trip, after my own loss, neither of us wanted to let go. I looked around for Gregg. He again was standing off to the side. But he looked so defeated. I knew that Deb would rationalize and compartmentalize her grief in order to deal with it. But it had to be especially hard for Gregg. He grew up as a minister's son, and he had relied on his faith to get him through some tough spots as he served his country. He knew that he could do his job and do it well, protecting those who needed it. *He's gotta know that God will now protect him and heal his heart.* He looked utterly lost. I tried not to start crying again.

Deb shared a particular poignant moment from the service. As the final prayers were being said on the side of the hill where Joey would remain, a butterfly landed on Les and stayed there until she got up to leave. She told me that one of Joey's favorite things to do was to chase butterflies. She said that Les saw it as a sign that Joey was now watching over her. I smiled. *Butterflies bring beauty and harmony to an otherwise uncertain world. With harmony comes peace. Please, God, send it their way!*

Chapter 27

You Can't Fix It

The following summer, I convinced Deb to come visit me. Gregg had actually called and begged me to help her understand that she needed to get away for a few days. When I saw her at the airport, she looked beaten. She looked like she could barely put one foot in front of the other. I was very afraid for her.

She wanted to rest, but she also wanted to visit with her brother in San Antonio, so we planned a quick road trip. We went by our old houses where we had spent so much time eons ago. We spent the night at her brother's house, visiting and catching up. I had also convinced her that we should go to the nearby outlet mall to shop, since that was one thing that she was born to do and do well, finding bargains wherever she went. It didn't even bring a small smile to her lips. I was beginning to feel totally helpless.

When we got back to the island that I now called home, Deb looked even worse that when she first got there. I thought that she only needed rest, but after two days of going through the motions, I decided to intervene. I went into the bedroom and lay down beside her. It finally came pouring out.

She told me that every time she closed her eyes, she relived it all over again. She saw Joey on the bed so still, with tubes everywhere. And the worse part for her was that she couldn't help her daughter or her grandbaby. She kept hearing Les begging Joey to come back, that they would play together every day, all day, if she just wouldn't leave. By this time, she was sobbing. She went on to tell me that at times, she had moments of understanding and thoughts of finally being able to work it out. But they were fleeting and elusive, and totally gone once she closed her eyes. She couldn't sleep, she couldn't grieve; she couldn't do anything but get up, help with the triplets, go home, and go to bed, where she would just lay staring up at the ceiling, waiting for anything to be different than the day before. Deb told me how powerless she felt and how angry she was at God for taking her too soon. *Have they both lost their faith?*

She cried for quite a while, and then gave a quiet laugh. She said something pretty profound, given the moment.

"This is just like *Steel Magnolias* when her best friend told Sally Field to "hit Wheezer!" We held each other, laughing and crying at the same time. I volunteered to whack her, and I got the I-double-dog-dare-you look. *Give it time, Deb. Just give it time.*

Her faith had always been so strong. I knew that eventually it would give her comfort. I just prayed that it would be much sooner than later.

Chapter 28

Or Can You?

Since 2007, I had not been feeling well. Two years later, numerous trips to the doctor yielded possible reasons, but not one treatment got me completely well. First it was my asthma getting worse. Then, perhaps it was my sleep apnea. I got a lot of suggestions to lose weight. My blood pressure kept slowly creeping up. I was becoming more frustrated and depressed, and it began to bubble over to other parts of my life. I found myself less and less interested in teaching. Nothing made me feel "right."

At Easter that year, I caught a mild case of pneumonia. Since my doctor lived on the island, and flu season was in full bloom, he decided that he really didn't want to put me in the hospital. Every day I drove the mile to his office for some kind of treatment or shot. After ten days, I was no better. Telling me that there was no way I could still have pneumonia with as much "crap" as he put in me, he arranged for me to have a C/T scan. It was there that my true problem was discovered.

I called my sister-in-law almost immediately. I knew she would find the way to break it to my brother. Sherry had always been quietly determined to do whatever had to be done, and I could almost hear the wheels turning, trying to make mental lists of all the things she needed to start getting prepared for. We talked for several minutes, and I pretended that it wasn't a big deal, knowing all along that we both knew that it was. I promised to call later that evening after I had time to gather my thoughts.

My second call was to Deb. Gregg answered. He knew something was up because I immediately asked to talk to her. We usually passed a few minutes of "small talk" before I asked to speak to Deb. But, not that day.

"Are you okay?" I heard the worry in his voice.

"I don't know." I was trying not to cry, but I was really scared.

I heard her ask in the background what was wrong. I heard his response. "I don't know but it doesn't sound good."

Deb got on the line. "What's going on?"

I took a deep breath. "I've got this little problem. Actually it is kind of a big problem." I knew she heard the cracks in my voice.

"You need to tell me what is happening," she demanded in her best mother voice. She knew about my pneumonia and the C/T.

"I have this aneurysm, and they want to do surgery on me pretty quick."

I heard her gasp. "An aneurysm? That cannot be good. Where?"

"In my aorta, near the heart. Deb, I am really afraid!" I was trying not to cry, but I was positive I was not doing a very good job of it. I had never been a part of a life threatening event directly involving me as the patient. I kept remembering how Mama handled herself in the face of death, and not only was I frightened, I was really afraid that everybody would compare my responses and behaviors to that of Mom, and that I would come up very short. It was a stupid thing, but I had always been the *care-giver* and not the *care-getter!* I didn't know how to act in this new role. I really needed help.

"When is your surgery?" I heard Deb sniffing, and I could imagine Gregg standing right next to her, his hand on her shoulder.

"I go to the surgeon next week, and then I'll know more. I still have to go see a heart doctor." I was really trying not to cry out loud.

"Well, you know I'll be there." I knew money was tight for them, so I tried to assure her that I would be alright, that she didn't have to come, all the while hoping that she would.

Gregg had been listening, and I heard his command. "You tell her that she has no say in this, that you are going, and I don't care how much it costs." I really cried then. I realized that in keeping Deb as my friend, I had also willingly inherited Gregg's friendship.

The next three weeks were frantically busy. Numerous trips to various doctors, procedures, heart catheterization, x-rays and blood draws occupied my days and my thoughts. Knowing that my artery could burst at any time, I became afraid to even move. I knew what had happened to the popular actor, John Ritter, and I was terribly afraid that I was heading down the same path. *Would they just find me lying on the floor one day? I don't want to die yet, and I don't want to be alone.* Not for the first time, I begged God to help me out and show me the way.

Sherry was finishing out the school year several hundred miles up the road, so I called my friend Jill daily to get her take on things. I then called Deb to check in with her and give updates on the latest happenings. After several conversations, Deb and I decided that Sherry and she should coordinate between the two of them as to who would be where and when they would get there. Jill would be their backup. At least they had a plan. Me? I was now the one in a fog.

I didn't know which way to turn. I was afraid to move. Every time my heart fluttered or my pulse pounded, I would ask if this was it. Then I would get angry for being so handicapped, and go out and do something totally irrational, only to have Jill remind me to calm down. I wanted it to be over, and I wanted it over then and there. I was not my momma, and I was not being brave! I wanted Deb there, but Sherry and she decided that she would come down a few days after the operation, when Sherry had to go back to work. My nephew was graduating from college at the other end of the state the weekend before my Monday morning date with the surgeon, and I made Sherry promise that she wouldn't miss that special moment. She made arrangements to drive down right after the ceremony. So I waited alone in my house, and I did an awful lot of soul searching and praying.

I began to think about what it would be like to die. Had I been good enough to be asked through the Pearly Gates? Had He forgiven me for all my wrongdoings? I knew I had done nothing majorly wrong, but what about all the little things that I did out of spite? Was my bad side ledger *waaay* longer than my good one? I thought about what my family would have to do if I died. I found an old spiral and began to list everything that I could think of that had to be attended to. I didn't have a will, so I wrote out my last wishes. Both Pete and Sherry knew that it was my desire to leave what little money would be left to their kids. I wrote copious and detailed instructions of my debts and people to contact. By the time Sherry got to my house the night before the surgery, I was calm on the outside, but very, very afraid on the inside.

The day of the operation was pretty much a blur. I suppose that was God's way of helping me cope. After the surgery, waking up in intensive care, I was acutely aware that I couldn't do anything but lie there and let the staff take care of me. Sleep was easier than being awake and wondering, so that was what I did. My only clear memory the first day was hearing Sherry's voice telling me not to talk because I had a tube down my throat. I remembered seeing Jill but not hearing her talk to me. Eventually I became more aware of my surroundings, but I pretty much blocked out all the comings and goings that occur in an intensive care ward. I had only one worry. *Is this the end of my ordeal, or is the end of my life still just right around the corner?*

Somehow through the grace of God, three strong women, and a really skilled surgeon, my aneurysm got fixed, and after a week in the hospital, I was able to come home to Deb's care. I had to be careful to not slip or reach up so as to keep the sternum in place as it healed. I completely submitted to her nursing. I was so glad that she had time to spend, since Sherry was busy doing all the things a counselor had to do to shut down the school for the summer.

Deb watched me like a hawk, letting me do what she thought I should do, and stopping me cold in my tracks with a "what are you doing?"

When she decided I had gone too far. I knew she could "mother" well, and I was now experiencing it up close and personal. She made me walk; she made me eat properly. It had been a long time since I had seen that takecharge side of her, and part of me was glad it was back. This was the Deb that I knew and loved.

She stayed with me for three weeks, and we both thanked God daily for having a world-renown thoracic surgeon in my corner. We talked about all the things that could have gone wrong, and how lucky I was to have a determined- to- find- the- answer kind of physician.

I sent my family doctor a thank you note telling him that he was the "Jethro Gibbs" of the medical field. He never gives up on a case, and he doesn't take no for an answer. Then I realized that he was pretty young, and might not watch *NCIS,* so I reminded him to ask one of the girls in the office if he didn't know about Mr. Gibbs. A few days later, I had to go in for a prescription and some blood work. He saw me and laughed.

I was getting a second chance. I had friends who cared. I had my best friend bossing me around and both of us loving every minute of it. My journey may have been considered a detour by many, but it was one that I was destined to travel. It was scary at times, and yet one of the most fulfilling trips of my life. I began to think of my future. I did not know what I was supposed to do, but I knew that He saved my life for a reason. *Boy! That is going to be some discovery trip!*

I again saw God's intervention. I realized that He had given me the will to not worry about tomorrow, as He would take care of me. All I had to do was let Him.

Just like my best friend, He would always be there...

Epilogue

October 2009

After Joey passed, her friends organized what has become one of the bigger events for the American Liver Foundation. To honor her life's journey and to raise funds and awareness for liver transplantation, they began an organization named *Joey Jog*. The first jog was held near Fairfax, Virginia, where Joey was born. The following year, it was held at Chapel Hill, in honor of the doctors at NC Children's Hospital that tried so desperately to save her life. The third and subsequent jogs would be held in Wilmington, her final home.

I had attended the first two, and was amazed at the number of people that joined the jog. Lots of money was raised the first time, and even more the second. I was really looking forward to see what would happen this year.

At each event, butterflies were released at the start of the walk/run. It was a powerful, yet beautiful, reminder of Joey. At both releases, one butterfly would always land on Les's shoulder and sit there for hours. Les would always laugh and tell us that Joey had come to visit her.

I really wanted to attend this third event, but my doctor decided that I wasn't ready to sit all day in airports and planes. He felt that I didn't need to be exposed to the flu bug that was still making people ill. I was disappointed, and I hated not being able to go, but understood his concerns. Both Deb and Les said that my health was more important that the jog, but that I definitely would be missed.

The day of the jog, the most unusual thing happened. I knew that we were on the monarch butterflies' fall and spring migration routes, and we very typically saw lots of them down here, but I was not prepared for the magnitude of what I witnessed.

Right about the time that the jog started, I looked outside. My eyes widened when I saw that almost the entire backyard was full of butterflies. I laughed. They stayed. In fact, they stayed for several hours. Then, about the time that the Joey Jog ended, the butterflies slowly, one or two at a time, flittered off.

When I talked with Deb later that afternoon, she was speechless. We both knew who had provided that miracle.

Life does indeed go on. Death is a part of it, but living is the important part. I knew that Deb, Les, and the rest of the family would eventually realize that it didn't hurt quite as much as yesterday, and that tomorrow might bring pure joy. Our friendship would survive, and Deb and I would now include Sherry, Jill, Les, and Abbey in our close-knit circle.

I smiled as I thought of Joey, Mom and Granny each holding on to her hands as she jumped clouds, her "beach." They would take good care of her.

Author's Note

This is a true story about friendship and coping with the everyday struggles that all people experience. Debbie and I have been friends our entire life, and we still marvel at how often our paths cross, even after all these years. We have been extremely fortunate in our friendship. Unfortunately, the story of Joey is also true, ft was a horrible time in their lives, one that they must deal with and come to terms with every single day. I hope that, with time, they all find peace through their love of family and their strong faith in God.

There are many people who encouraged me along the way to tell this story. Thank you, Debbie, Jill, Sherry, and Gail. I am glad that you all spell better than me! Thank you, Les and Andre for allowing me to include your personal moments in this story. Thank you, Pete, for showing me how much you love me. And especially, thank you, Joey, for bringing so much joy to so many people during your short stay with us.

If you would like more information on how you can help fund research or families awaiting a transplant for their loved one, please visit: The local office of the American Liver Foundation.

About the Author

Cynthia is an eighth generation Texan who grew up in San Antonio and the Hill Country. After working many years in banking, she went back to school and earned her teaching certificate. Twenty-two years later, she decided to retire and enjoy beach living on North Padre Island, just outside Corpus Christi. She likes to fish, even though she is not very good at. Her favorite past time is watching people and birds while sitting in her beach chair along the shore. Cynthia and her friend Debbie are currently collaborating on a series of children's books based on their many misadventures.

Milton Keynes UK
Ingram Content Group UK Ltd.
UKHW020224210824
447185UK00001B/123